THIS BOOK BELONGS TO

The Library of

....

Did you like my book? I pondered it severely before releasing this book. Although the response has been overwhelming, it is always pleasing to see, read or hear a new comment. Thank you for reading this and I would love to hear your honest opinion about it. Furthermore, many people are searching for a unique book, and your feedback will help me gather the right books for my reading audience.

Thanks!

Table of Contents

SUMMARY

Embracing the Charm of Crochet Ragdolls: Crochet ragdolls have a unique charm that is hard to resist. These adorable handmade toys are not only fun to make, but they also make wonderful gifts for children and adults alike. The art of crocheting ragdolls has been around for centuries, and it continues to captivate crafters and enthusiasts around the world.

One of the reasons why crochet ragdolls are so charming is the level of detail that can be achieved through this craft. With just a hook and some yarn, skilled crocheters can create intricate patterns and designs that bring these dolls to life. From the delicate facial features to the tiny clothing and accessories, every aspect of a crochet ragdoll can be customized to reflect the creator's imagination and creativity.

Another aspect that adds to the charm of crochet ragdolls is the nostalgia they evoke. These dolls often remind us of our childhood and the toys we cherished. They have a timeless appeal that transcends generations, making them a beloved keepsake that can be passed down from one family member to another. Crochet ragdolls have a way of bringing back fond memories and creating new ones, making them a cherished companion for both young and old.

Furthermore, crochet ragdolls offer a sense of warmth and comfort. The softness of the yarn and the handmade nature of these dolls make them perfect for cuddling and snuggling. They provide a sense of security and companionship, especially for children who may find solace in having a special toy to confide in or play with. The love and care that goes into creating a crochet ragdoll can be felt in every stitch, making them a source of comfort and joy.

In addition to their charm, crochet ragdolls also offer a creative outlet for crafters. The process of crocheting allows for endless possibilities in terms of design and customization. From choosing the colors and types of yarn to adding personal touches like embroidered details or embellishments, crocheters can truly make each ragdoll a unique work of art. This creative freedom not only makes the crafting process enjoyable but also allows for a sense of accomplishment and pride in the finished product.

Overall, embracing the charm of crochet ragdolls is a delightful experience. These handmade toys bring joy, nostalgia, and comfort to both the creator and the recipient. Whether you are a seasoned crocheter or a beginner looking to explore a new craft, crocheting ragdolls is a rewarding and fulfilling endeavor.

Selecting the Right Materials for Softness and Durability of Crochet Ragdolls: When it comes to creating crochet ragdolls, selecting the right materials is crucial to achieve the perfect balance of softness and durability. The choice of materials not only affects the overall feel of the finished product but also determines its longevity and ability to withstand regular play and handling.

One of the key factors to consider when selecting materials for crochet ragdolls is the softness of the yarn. Softness is essential as it ensures that the ragdoll is comfortable to touch and cuddle. It also adds to the overall appeal of the toy, making it more inviting for children to play with. Opting for yarns made from natural fibers such as cotton or bamboo can provide a soft and gentle texture, perfect for creating a cozy and huggable ragdoll.

In addition to softness, durability is equally important to ensure that the crochet ragdoll can withstand the wear and tear of regular play. Choosing yarns that are strong and resistant to fraying or breaking is essential. Acrylic yarns, for example, are known for their durability and ability to maintain their shape even after repeated use. They are also easy to care for, making them a practical choice for crochet ragdolls that are likely to be handled by children.

Another aspect to consider when selecting materials for crochet ragdolls is the safety of the toy. It is crucial to choose yarns that are free from harmful chemicals and toxins, especially if the ragdoll is intended for young children. Opting for yarns that are certified as safe for children's toys can provide peace of mind and ensure that the finished product is safe for play.

Furthermore, the choice of materials can also impact the overall aesthetic of the crochet ragdoll. Different yarns come in a variety of colors, textures, and finishes, allowing for endless creative possibilities. Considering the desired look and feel of the ragdoll can help in selecting the right materials that align with the intended design.

In conclusion, selecting the right materials for softness and durability is crucial when creating crochet ragdolls. The choice of yarns can greatly impact the overall feel, longevity, and safety of the finished product. By considering factors such as softness, durability, safety, and aesthetic appeal, one can ensure that the crochet ragdoll is not only a joy to play with but also a cherished keepsake that can withstand the test of time.

The Joy of Creating and Sharing Crochet Ragdolls: The Joy of Creating and Sharing Crochet Ragdolls is a delightful and fulfilling experience that brings together the art of crochet and the joy of sharing handmade creations. Crochet ragdolls, also known as amigurumi, are adorable stuffed toys made using crochet techniques. They are often designed to resemble animals, characters, or even mythical creatures, and can be customized to reflect the creator's imagination and creativity.

The process of creating crochet ragdolls is not only a creative outlet but also a therapeutic activity. As you work with your hands, manipulating the yarn and crochet hook, you enter a state of flow where your mind becomes fully engaged in the present moment. This meditative quality of crochet allows you to relax, reduce stress, and find solace in the repetitive motions of stitching. The rhythmic nature of crochet also has a calming effect, making it an ideal hobby for those seeking a mindful and soothing activity.

Furthermore, the joy of creating crochet ragdolls extends beyond the act of crafting itself. Once completed, these adorable creations can be shared with loved ones, gifted to friends, or even donated to charitable organizations. The act of giving a handmade ragdoll to someone brings immense joy and warmth, as it is a tangible expression of love and care. The recipient of a crochet ragdoll is not only receiving a unique and one-of-a-kind gift but also a piece of the creator's heart and soul.

Moreover, the process of sharing crochet ragdolls goes beyond personal connections. Many crochet enthusiasts choose to share their creations with the wider community through social media platforms, online forums, or even by selling their patterns or finished products. By sharing their work, these individuals inspire and encourage others to embark on their own creative journeys. The crochet community is a vibrant and supportive one, where members cheer each other on, offer advice and tips, and celebrate each other's accomplishments. The act of sharing crochet ragdolls not only brings joy to the creator but also fosters a sense of belonging and camaraderie within the community.

In addition to the emotional and social benefits, creating and sharing crochet ragdolls also allows for personal growth and skill development. As you embark on different projects, you learn new crochet techniques, experiment with different stitches, and expand your repertoire of skills. Each ragdoll becomes an opportunity to challenge yourself, push your creative boundaries, and improve your craftsmanship.

Essential Tools and Materials of Crochet Ragdolls: When it comes to creating crochet ragdolls, there are a few essential tools and materials that you will need to have on hand. These items are crucial for ensuring that your ragdoll turns out beautifully and that the process of creating it goes smoothly.

First and foremost, you will need a set of crochet hooks. These hooks come in various sizes, and the size you choose will depend on the thickness of the yarn you plan to use. It's a good idea to have a range of hook sizes available, as different parts of the ragdoll may require different hook sizes to achieve the desired tension and stitch definition.

Next, you will need yarn. The type of yarn you choose will greatly impact the final look and feel of your ragdoll. Acrylic yarn is a popular choice for crochet ragdolls, as it is affordable, easy to work with, and comes in a wide range of colors. However, you can also experiment with other types of yarn, such as cotton or wool, to achieve different textures and effects.

In addition to crochet hooks and yarn, you will also need a few other tools to complete your crochet ragdoll. One essential tool is a pair of scissors for cutting the yarn. It's important to have a sharp pair of scissors that can easily cut through the yarn without fraying or damaging it.

Another tool that you may find useful is a yarn needle. This needle is used for weaving in loose ends and sewing different parts of the ragdoll together. A yarn needle with a large eye is ideal, as it will make threading the yarn easier.

Furthermore, you may want to have a stitch marker on hand. This small tool is used to mark the beginning of a round or a specific stitch, making it easier to keep track of your progress and prevent mistakes.

Lastly, having a tape measure or ruler is essential for ensuring that your ragdoll is the correct size. This tool will help you measure the length and width of different parts of the ragdoll, such as the arms, legs, and body, to ensure that they are consistent and proportional.

In conclusion, creating crochet ragdolls requires a few essential tools and materials. These include crochet hooks, yarn, scissors, a yarn needle, a stitch marker, and a tape measure or ruler. By having these items on hand, you will be well-equipped to embark on your crochet ragdoll journey and create beautiful, handmade creations.

Basic Stitches and Techniques for Ragdoll Crochet: In this tutorial, we will explore the basic stitches and techniques that are commonly used in ragdoll crochet. Ragdoll crochet is a popular form of amigurumi, which involves creating adorable stuffed dolls using crochet techniques. Whether you are a beginner or an experienced crocheter, mastering these basic stitches and techniques will help you create beautiful and intricate ragdoll designs.

The first stitch we will cover is the chain stitch. This stitch forms the foundation of your crochet project and is used to create a starting row. To make a chain stitch, simply yarn over and pull the yarn through the loop on your hook. Repeat this process until you have the desired number of chains. The chain stitch is often used to create the limbs and body of a ragdoll.

Next, we have the single crochet stitch. This stitch is commonly used in amigurumi projects as it creates a tight and sturdy fabric. To make a single crochet stitch, insert your hook into the next stitch, yarn over, and pull the yarn through the stitch. Yarn over again and pull through both loops on your hook. Repeat this process for each stitch in the row. The single crochet stitch is perfect for creating the head and body of your ragdoll.

Moving on, we have the double crochet stitch. This stitch is slightly taller than the single crochet stitch and creates a looser fabric. To make a double crochet stitch, yarn over, insert your hook into the next stitch, yarn over again, and pull the yarn through the stitch. Yarn over once more and pull through the first two loops on your hook. Yarn over again and pull through the remaining two loops. The double crochet stitch is often used to create decorative elements such as hair or clothing for your ragdoll.

Another important technique in ragdoll crochet is increasing and decreasing stitches. Increasing stitches allows you to add more stitches in a row, while decreasing stitches helps shape your project. To increase, simply make two stitches in the same stitch. To decrease, crochet two stitches together. These techniques are crucial for creating the curves and contours of your ragdoll's body and limbs.

Lastly, we have the magic ring technique. This technique is used to create a tight and seamless starting point for crocheting in the round. To make a magic ring, wrap the yarn around your fingers, insert your hook under the first loop, and pull the yarn through. Then, chain one and make the desired number of stitches into the ring.

Understanding Ragdoll Patterns and Assembly of Crochet Ragdolls

Crochet ragdolls are adorable and versatile toys that can be made using various patterns and techniques. To successfully create a crochet ragdoll, it is essential to have a good understanding of ragdoll patterns and the assembly process.

Ragdoll patterns are essentially the blueprint or guide that helps you create a crochet ragdoll. These patterns provide detailed instructions on the stitches, techniques, and materials required to make the ragdoll. They also include information on the size, shape, and design of the doll, allowing you to customize it according to your preferences.

When choosing a ragdoll pattern, it is important to consider your skill level and experience in crocheting. Some patterns may be more suitable for beginners, while others may require advanced techniques and skills. It is advisable to start with simpler patterns if you are a beginner and gradually progress to more complex ones as you gain confidence and expertise.

Once you have selected a pattern, it is time to gather the necessary materials. The materials required for crocheting a ragdoll typically include yarn, crochet hooks, stuffing, safety eyes or buttons for the doll's eyes, and a yarn needle for sewing and assembly. It is important to choose high-quality materials that are soft, durable, and safe for children, especially if the ragdoll is intended as a toy.

Before starting the crocheting process, it is crucial to read and understand the pattern thoroughly. Pay attention to the abbreviations and symbols used in the pattern, as they indicate specific stitches and techniques. Familiarize yourself with the different types of stitches, such as single crochet, double crochet, and slip stitch, as they are commonly used in ragdoll patterns.

Once you are familiar with the pattern and have gathered all the materials, you can begin crocheting the ragdoll. Follow the instructions step by step, ensuring that you maintain the correct tension and gauge throughout the project. Tension refers to the tightness or looseness of your stitches, while gauge refers to the number of stitches and rows per inch. Both tension and gauge play a crucial role in achieving the desired size and shape of the ragdoll.

As you crochet the different parts of the ragdoll, such as the head, body, arms, and legs, make sure to stuff them with the appropriate amount of stuffing. The stuffing gives the doll its shape and makes it soft and cuddly.

Finishing Techniques for a Professional Look of Crochet Ragdolls: When it comes to creating crochet ragdolls, the finishing techniques play a crucial role in achieving a professional and polished look. These techniques not only enhance the overall appearance of the doll but also ensure that it is durable and long-lasting. In this article, we will explore some of the key finishing techniques that can be employed to elevate your crochet ragdolls to the next level.

One of the first finishing techniques to consider is the use of invisible or seamless joins. This technique involves joining different parts of the doll, such as the head, body, arms, and legs, in a way that creates a seamless and smooth transition. By using this technique, you can avoid any visible gaps or bumps that may detract from the overall aesthetic of the doll. There are various methods to achieve invisible joins, such as the slip stitch join or the mattress stitch, and it is important to experiment and find the one that works best for your specific project.

Another important finishing technique is the incorporation of facial features. The face of a crochet ragdoll is what brings it to life and gives it its unique personality. Whether you choose to embroider the eyes, nose, and mouth or use safety eyes and a plastic nose, it is crucial to pay attention to the placement and symmetry of these features. Taking the time to carefully position and secure the facial features will ensure that your ragdoll has a professional and appealing appearance.

Additionally, the choice of yarn and color selection can greatly impact the final look of your crochet ragdoll. Opting for high-quality yarn that is soft and durable will not only make the doll more comfortable to touch but also enhance its overall appearance. Furthermore, selecting the right colors for the different parts of the doll, such as the hair, clothing, and accessories, can add depth and dimension to the finished product. Consider using a color palette that complements the overall theme or character of the ragdoll to create a cohesive and visually pleasing result.

Furthermore, paying attention to the details is crucial in achieving a professional finish. This includes techniques such as stuffing the doll evenly and firmly to ensure a consistent shape, as well as properly securing any loose ends or yarn tails. Taking the time to weave in these ends and hide them within the stitches will give your ragdoll a polished and seamless look.

Lastly, blocking and shaping the finished doll can greatly enhance its appearance. Blocking involves wetting the doll and then reshaping it to achieve a more defined and symmetrical form.

Personalizing Your Ragdoll with Accessories in Crochet Ragdolls: When it comes to creating crochet ragdolls, one of the most exciting aspects is personalizing them with accessories. Adding accessories not only enhances the overall appearance of the ragdoll but also allows you to infuse your own creativity and style into the finished product.

There are countless options when it comes to choosing accessories for your crochet ragdoll. From hats and scarves to bows and bags, the possibilities are endless. You can opt for simple and classic accessories or go for more elaborate and unique ones, depending on your preference and the personality you want to give to your ragdoll.

One popular accessory for crochet ragdolls is a hat. Hats can instantly transform the look of your ragdoll and give it a distinct character. You can choose from a wide range of hat styles, such as beanies, berets, or even sun hats. Additionally, you can experiment with different colors and patterns to make the hat truly stand out.

Scarves are another fantastic accessory to consider. They not only add a touch of warmth and coziness to your ragdoll but also provide an opportunity to play with different textures and yarns. You can create a long, flowing scarf or a shorter, chunky one, depending on the style you want to achieve. Adding fringe or tassels can also add a fun and playful element to the scarf.

Bows are a great accessory for adding a feminine touch to your crochet ragdoll. You can attach a bow to the hair or even use it as a decorative element on the ragdoll's clothing. Bows can be made in various sizes and colors, allowing you to customize them to match the overall look of your ragdoll.

If you want to take the accessorizing game to the next level, consider adding bags or purses to your crochet ragdoll. These miniature accessories can be made using different crochet techniques, such as amigurumi or tapestry crochet. You can create tiny backpacks, tote bags, or even handbags, giving your ragdoll a stylish and fashionable look.

When personalizing your crochet ragdoll with accessories, it's important to consider the overall theme or concept you have in mind. For example, if you're creating a winter-themed ragdoll, you might want to add a hat and scarf in cozy, wintery colors. On the other hand, if you're going for a more whimsical or fantasy-inspired look, you can experiment with vibrant colors and unique accessories like wings or crowns.

Care Instructions for Longevity and Safety of Crochet Ragdolls

Crochet ragdolls are not only adorable and cuddly, but they also require proper care to ensure their longevity and safety. By following these care instructions, you can keep your crochet ragdolls in excellent condition for years to come.

1. Gentle Handwashing: To clean your crochet ragdoll, it is best to handwash it using mild detergent and lukewarm water. Avoid using harsh chemicals or bleach as they can damage the delicate fibers of the doll. Gently lather the doll and rinse it thoroughly to remove any soap residue. Avoid wringing or twisting the doll as it can distort its shape.

2. Air Drying: After washing, gently squeeze out excess water from the doll and lay it flat on a clean towel to air dry. Avoid using a dryer or exposing the doll to direct sunlight as it can cause fading or shrinkage. Allow the doll to dry completely before handling or storing it.

3. Brushing and Detangling: Over time, the yarn fibers of the crochet ragdoll may become tangled or matted. To keep the doll looking its best, gently brush or comb through the yarn using a soft-bristled brush or a wide-toothed comb. Start from the top and work your way down, being careful not to pull or tug on the yarn.

4. Storage: When not in use, it is important to store your crochet ragdoll properly to prevent damage. Place the doll in a clean, dry storage container or a breathable fabric bag to protect it from dust and dirt. Avoid storing the doll in plastic bags or airtight containers as they can trap moisture and lead to mold or mildew growth.

5. Avoid Rough Play: While crochet ragdolls are designed to be played with, it is important to avoid rough play or pulling on the doll's limbs. Excessive pulling or tugging can cause the yarn to unravel or the stitches to come loose, compromising the doll's structural integrity. Encourage gentle play and supervise young children when they are handling the doll.

6. Repairing: If you notice any loose stitches or damage to your crochet ragdoll, it is best to repair it as soon as possible. Use a needle and matching yarn to carefully stitch up any loose stitches or tears. If the damage is extensive, consider seeking professional help from a skilled crochet artist or doll repair specialist.

Adapting Ragdoll Patterns for Different Age Groups in Crochet Ragdolls: When it comes to creating crochet ragdolls, one of the key factors to consider is the age group for which the doll is intended. Different age groups have varying needs and preferences, and it is important to adapt the patterns accordingly to ensure that the ragdoll is safe, enjoyable, and appropriate for the intended recipient.

For younger children, particularly infants and toddlers, safety is of utmost importance. It is crucial to avoid using any small parts or embellishments that could pose a choking hazard. Additionally, the doll should be made using soft and washable materials, as young children tend to put toys in their mouths and may also have accidents that require frequent cleaning. The size of the doll should also be taken into consideration, as it should be easy for small hands to grasp and carry around.

As children grow older, their interests and abilities change. For preschoolers and early school-age children, incorporating educational elements into the ragdoll can be a great way to engage their curiosity and promote learning through play. This can be done by adding features such as removable clothing with buttons, zippers, or snaps, which can help develop fine motor skills and encourage independent dressing. Including different textures and colors in the design can also stimulate sensory exploration and cognitive development.

For older children and teenagers, the focus may shift towards creating ragdolls that reflect their personal interests and hobbies. This can be achieved by customizing the doll's appearance, such as adding accessories or clothing that represent a favorite sport, hobby, or fictional character. Additionally, more complex patterns and techniques can be used to challenge and engage older children who have developed more advanced crochet skills.

In addition to age considerations, it is also important to take into account the preferences and needs of individuals with special needs. For example, for children with sensory sensitivities, using soft and hypoallergenic yarns can help prevent any discomfort or irritation. For children with limited mobility or dexterity, adapting the pattern to include larger and easier-to-grasp features can enhance their ability to interact with the ragdoll.

Overall, adapting ragdoll patterns for different age groups requires careful consideration of safety, developmental appropriateness, and individual needs. By taking these factors into account, crochet enthusiasts can create ragdolls that are not only visually appealing but also engaging, educational, and enjoyable for children of all ages.

Interactive Features for Added Play Value of Crochet Ragdolls: Interactive features can greatly enhance the play value of crochet ragdolls, providing children with a more engaging and immersive play experience. These features can range from simple additions, such as removable clothing and accessories, to more complex mechanisms like sound or motion.

One popular interactive feature is the inclusion of removable clothing and accessories. This allows children to dress up their ragdolls in different outfits, fostering creativity and imaginative play. They can mix and match different pieces of clothing, creating unique looks for their dolls. Additionally, removable accessories like hats, shoes, and bags can be added to further enhance the play value and provide more opportunities for customization.

Another interactive feature that can be incorporated into crochet ragdolls is sound. This can be achieved by adding a small sound module or speaker inside the doll. When certain parts of the doll are pressed or squeezed, it can produce sounds like giggles, cries, or even phrases. This feature adds an element of surprise and delight for children, as they can interact with their dolls in a more dynamic way.

Motion is another exciting interactive feature that can be integrated into crochet ragdolls. This can be achieved by incorporating mechanisms like joints or movable limbs. These mechanisms allow the doll to be posed in different positions, enabling children to create various scenes and scenarios during playtime. For example, a doll with movable arms can be made to wave or hug, adding a realistic touch to the play experience.

Furthermore, interactive features can also be educational. For instance, some crochet ragdolls can be designed with buttons or zippers that children can practice manipulating, helping them develop fine motor skills. Additionally, dolls can be made with different textures or sensory elements, providing tactile stimulation and promoting sensory exploration.

In conclusion, interactive features greatly enhance the play value of crochet ragdolls. Whether it's through removable clothing and accessories, sound, motion, or educational elements, these features provide children with a more immersive and engaging play experience. By incorporating these interactive features, crochet ragdolls become more than just toys; they become companions that inspire creativity, imagination, and learning.

The Role of Ragdolls in Emotional Development in Crochet Ragdolls: The role of ragdolls in emotional development in crochet ragdolls is a fascinating and important aspect to consider. Ragdolls, with their soft and huggable nature, have been a beloved toy for children for generations. However, their impact on emotional development goes beyond just being a cuddly companion.

Firstly, ragdolls provide a sense of comfort and security to children. The soft texture and familiar presence of a ragdoll can help soothe a child during times of stress or anxiety. This can be particularly beneficial for children who may struggle with separation anxiety or have difficulty expressing their emotions. The act of hugging or holding a ragdoll can provide a sense of reassurance and stability, helping children to feel safe and supported.

In addition to providing comfort, ragdolls also play a role in fostering empathy and nurturing skills in children. Through imaginative play, children can project their own emotions onto the ragdoll, allowing them to explore and understand different feelings. This can help children develop empathy towards others, as they learn to recognize and respond to the emotions of their ragdoll companion. Furthermore, caring for a ragdoll by dressing it, feeding it, or even pretending to take it to the doctor, can help children develop nurturing skills and a sense of responsibility.

Moreover, ragdolls can serve as a tool for communication and self-expression. Children often use their ragdolls as a means to express their thoughts and feelings, especially when they may struggle to articulate them verbally. By engaging in pretend play with their ragdoll, children can act out scenarios and explore different emotions in a safe and non-judgmental environment. This can be particularly beneficial for children who may be shy or have difficulty expressing themselves, as it provides them with a creative outlet to communicate and process their emotions.

Furthermore, the process of creating a crochet ragdoll can also contribute to emotional development. The act of crocheting requires patience, focus, and attention to detail, which can help children develop important skills such as perseverance and problem-solving. Additionally, the sense of accomplishment and pride that comes from completing a crochet ragdoll can boost a child's self-esteem and confidence.

In conclusion, the role of ragdolls in emotional development in crochet ragdolls is multifaceted and significant. From providing comfort and security to fostering empathy and nurturing skills, ragdolls play a crucial role in supporting children's emotional well-being.

CROCHET
STITCHES

Chain	ch
Slip stitch	sl st
Single crochet	sc
Half double crochet	hdc
Double crochet	dc
Triple crochet	tr
Single crochet 2 together	sc2tog
Double crochet 2 together	dc2tog
Front post double crochet	fpdc
Back post double crochet	bpdc

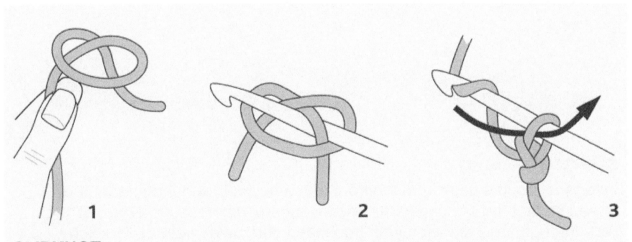

SLIPKNOT

Your crochet (usually) starts with a slipknot and chain stitches. Lay the loose end of your thread over the thread that is attached to the ball of yarn, and then fold it down behind the loop (1). Now insert your crochet hook into the ring and behind the end, then forward again (2). Tighten the thread, and you have made a slipknot. You can now work the setup chain by hooking through the loop on your hook (3).

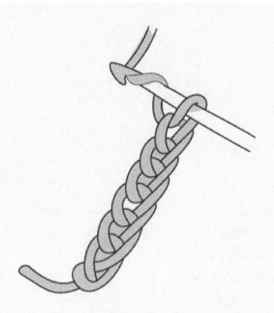

CHAIN (ch)

Wrap the working yarn from back to front over the crochet hook. Now pull the yarn through the loop on your hook, and you have made a chain stitch. Repeat for the desired number of chains.

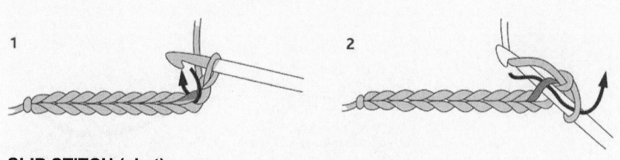

SLIP STITCH (sl st)

Insert the crochet hook from the front to the back (1) and then under the thread so that the working yarn is over your crochet hook (2). Now pull the yarn through the 2 loops on your hook, and you have made a slip stitch.

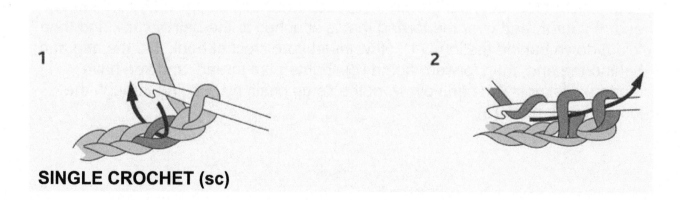

SINGLE CROCHET (sc)

Insert the crochet hook from the front to the back (1) and wrap the working yarn over the hook from back to front. Now pull the yarn through the stitch. Wrap the yarn over the hook from back to front again and pull this through the 2 loops on your hook (2), and you have made a single crochet.

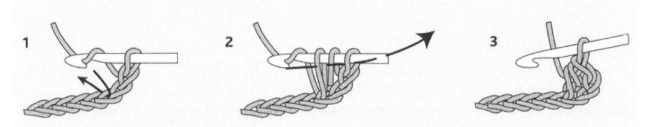

HALF DOUBLE CROCHET (hdc)

Wrap the working yarn from back to front over the crochet hook (1). Insert the crochet hook from the front to the back, wrap the working yarn over the hook from back to front, and then pull the yarn through the stitch. Make another wrap and pass it through the 3 loops on your hook (2), and you have made a half double crochet (3).

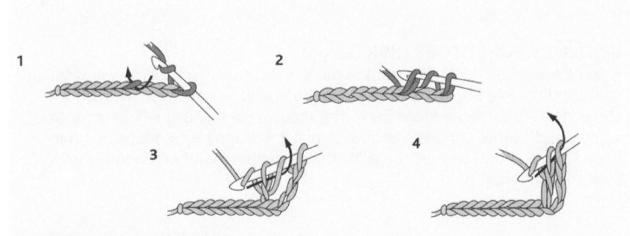

DOUBLE CROCHET (dc)

Wrap the working yarn from back to front over the crochet hook (1). Insert the crochet hook from the front to the back, wrap the yarn over the hook, and then pull the yarn through the stitch (2). Make another wrap and pass it through 2 of the loops on your hook (3). Then make another wrap and pull it through the last 2 loops on your hook (4), and you have made a double crochet.

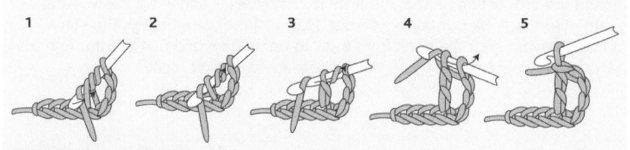

TRIPLE CROCHET (tr)

Wrap the yarn around the crochet hook 2 times from back to front. Insert the crochet hook from the front to the back, make a wrap and pull the yarn through the stitch (1), *make another wrap and pull it through 2 of the loops on your hook* (2), repeat from * to * 2 more times (3 and 4), and you have made a triple crochet (5).

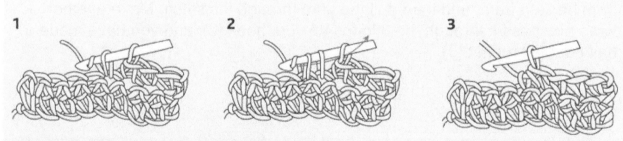

SINGLE CROCHET TOGETHER (sctog)

Insert the crochet hook from front to back in the next stitch. Wrap the working yarn from back to front over the crochet hook and pull the yarn through the stitch (1). Repeat these steps for the next stitch (or multiple stitches that you want to join). Finally, make a wrap and pull it through all the loops on your hook (2). You now have crocheted several stitches together, decreasing the total stitch count (3).

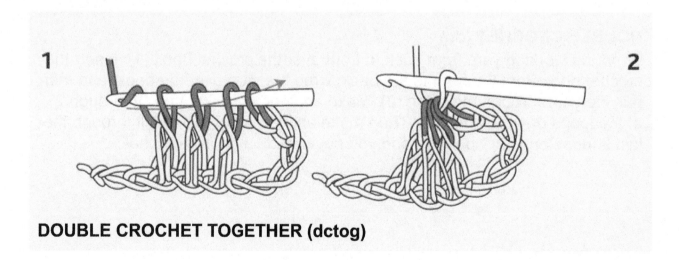

DOUBLE CROCHET TOGETHER (dctog)

Wrap the working yarn from back to front over the crochet hook. Insert the crochet hook from the front to the back in the next stitch. Make a wrap and pull it through the stitch, and then make another wrap and pull it through 2 of the loops on your hook. Repeat these steps for the next or possibly several stitches that you want to join. Finally, make a wrap and pull it through all the loops on your hook (1). You have now double crocheted several stitches together to make 1 stitch (2).

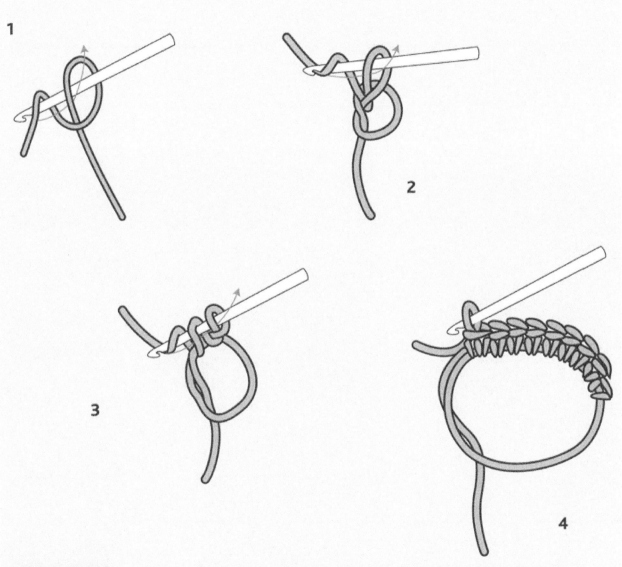

MAGIC RING

Make a circle of the yarn by folding the loose end of the yarn behind the yarn attached to the skein. Now insert your crochet hook into the ring. Wrap the working yarn over your hook and pull the yarn through the ring (1). Hook 1 chain to secure the ring (2).

Then hook the number of stitches in the ring as indicated in the pattern. Make sure that you hook around the strands of both the ring and the loose end of the yarn (3 and 4). When you have the desired number of stitches, pull the loose end tightly to close the ring. Then continue in pattern.

YARN
CHOICES

All the sample animals are crocheted with Scheepjes Stone Washed. This is a yarn with a special soft, tonal appearance with few equivalents. However, you can use other yarns and brands to crochet the dolls. On this page and the following, you'll see examples of the same pattern crocheted in different yarns. Try any of these yarns, or make your own choices from your stash or local craft store.

All these ragdolls are crocheted with a US size D-3 (3 mm) crochet hook, but, as you can see, each yarn has its own effect and the finished ragdolls also vary in size!

1 Scheepjes Stone Washed: recommended hook size US D-3–F-5 (3–4 mm); 78% cotton, 22% acrylic; 1.75 oz. (50 g); 142 yd. (130 m) per ball. This yarn makes the ragdoll 14.2 in. (36 cm) high and the body 5.9 in. (15 cm) wide.

2 Annell Miami or Scheepjes Soft Fun: recommended hook size US D-3–E-4 (3–3.5 mm); 60% cotton, 40% acrylic; 1.75 oz. (50 g); 153 yd. (140 m)

per ball. This yarn makes the ragdoll 15 in. (38 cm) high and the body 6.3 in. (16 cm) wide.

3. SMC Merino Extrafine 120: recommended hook size US D-3–F-5 (3–4 mm); 100% new milled wool; 1.75 oz. (50 g); 131.2 yd. (120 m) per ball. This yarn makes the ragdoll 13.4 in. (34 cm) high and the body 5.1 in. (13 cm) wide.

4. Lammy Jeans: recommended hook size US E-4–G-6 (3.5–4 mm); 100% cotton; 1.75 oz. (50 g); 153 yd. (140 m) per ball. This yarn makes the ragdoll 14.2 in. (36 cm) high and the body 5.5 in. (14 cm) wide.

5. SMC Catania Grande: recommended hook size US G-6–H-8 (4–5 mm); 100% cotton; 1.75 oz. (50 g); 68.9 yd. (63 m) per ball. This yarn makes the ragdoll 16.9 in. (43 cm) high and the body 6.3 in. (16 cm) wide. This yarn is thicker than the other yarns, so you can also use a slightly thicker crochet hook US size E-4/F-5/G-6 (3.5–5 mm), and your ragdoll will become a little larger.

TIPS &
TRICKS

1. You crochet a lot of parts in continuous rounds; it is therefore useful to use a stitch marker.

2. To change colors, work the last step of the stitch before the color change. For example, if the last stitch in the old color is a single crochet, work the last wrap over the hook that you then pull through 2 loops.

3. With a number of the patterns, you change colors regularly. Instead of fastening off every time, carry the unused color along. You do this by holding the color that you are not using along the top of the stitches to be crocheted and hooking around it so that it is encased by the working color and hidden on the back of the work.

4. You can add sounds to the ragdolls to give them an extra play element. For example, put a squeaker in the head of the mouse, a bell in the head of the cat, a rattle bead in a hand, or a sheet of crisp plastic in the body.

5. Safety eyes should only be used on ragdolls meant for children over the age of three. When making a ragdoll for a younger child, please replace with crocheted or embroidered eyes for optimal safety.

6. Here are some tips for making the body:
   - The body is worked in the round. You'll start with a chain on which you'll crochet along both sides to begin the top of the body.
   - You'll always start with a ch2, which doesn't count as the first dc, so the actual first dc will be made in the same stitch as the ch2.
   - Your increases should stack on top of each other.
   - Depending on how tight you crochet, the body may twist a little. But in the end, you can fold it flat in line with the increases and sew in place.
   - When working a two-color body, you'll notice that the increases of the second color will be made only on one side. This is because when you crochet in the round, your stitches automatically turn to the right, so this will make the belly look even.

SKILL LEVELS

 Beginner

Advanced beginner

Intermediate

Advanced intermediate

Advanced

38

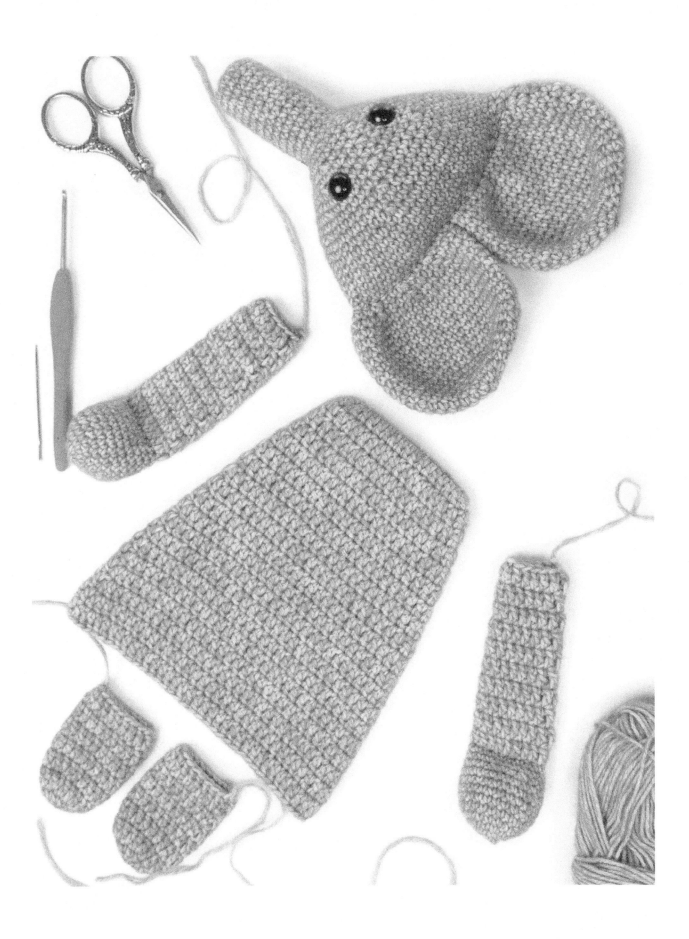

ASSEMBLY

The dolls all have the same basic construction. The patterns themselves describe in detail how to assemble each specific one, but here are some general instructions including photos.

CROCHETING THE HEAD

All the heads are crocheted in the round, but in a number of different ways. The simplest patterns start with a magic ring or a chain around which you then continue to crochet in the round. Another way is to start crocheting two eyes or two ears that you then hook together in one row to form the top of the head. Or you can start with the top component, such as the eyes or a bun, and then make a chain between or beside it; then you continue to crochet around all stitches.

PLACING THE LEGS AND TAIL (IF ONE)

It is very important that you fold the body so that the belly is in the middle. This is especially important with the dolls that have a white belly. Take the body and place both legs (and possibly the tail) between the two layers at the bottom; then sew the bottom of the body with the remaining yarn and at the same time attach the parts.

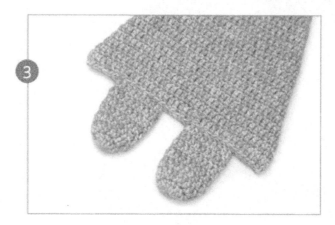

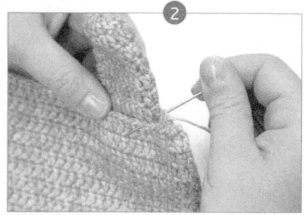

ATTACHING THE ARMS

Sew an arm on either side of the upper rounds of the body. The precise rounds will be indicated in the pattern.

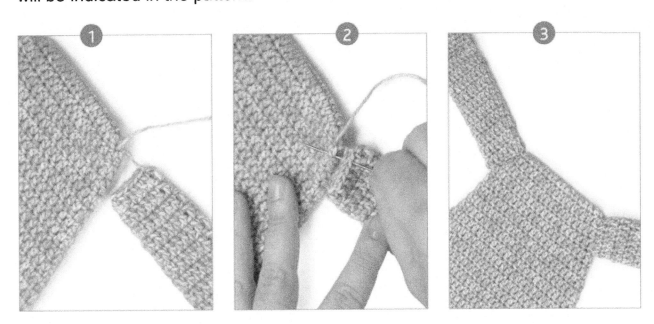

ATTACHING THE HEAD

Finally, sew the back of the head to the body through both layers. The precise rounds will be indicated in the pattern.

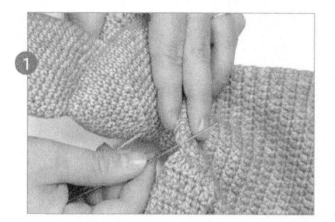

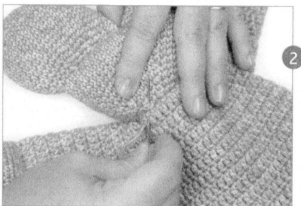

ANIMAL
FAMILIES

BUNNY

This bunny loves to sniff and cuddle.

18.1 in. (46 cm) high (with ears) and 6.7 in. (17 cm) wide

MATERIALS

DK #3 lightweight yarn (sample shown in Scheepjes
Stone Washed):
• gray (Smokey Quartz): 251.5 yd. (230 m)
• white (Moon Stone): 142.2 yd. (130 m)
Crochet hook: US size D-3 (3 mm)
Black and brown safety eyes, 15 mm
Safety nose, 15 mm wide
Fiberfill stuffing
Yarn needle and scissors

DIFFICULTY LEVEL

EARS (MAKE 2)

Rnd 1: With gray, start with a magic ring, ch2, 6dc in the ring, sl st in first dc. (6)
Rnd 2: Ch2 (doesn't count as first stitch now and throughout), 2dc in each stitch around, sl st in first dc. (12)
Rnd 3: Ch2, *dc1, 2dc in next*, repeat from * to * around, sl st in first dc. (18)
Rnd 4: Ch2, *dc2, 2dc in next*, repeat from * to * around, sl st in first dc. (24)
Rnd 5–Rnd 7: Ch2, dc1 in each stitch around, sl st in first dc. (24)
Rnd 8: Ch2, *dc2, dc2tog*, repeat from * to * around, sl st in first dc. (18)
Rnd 9–Rnd 16: Ch2, dc1 in each stitch around, sl st in first dc. (18)
Cut yarn of first ear, but don't cut yarn of second ear because you'll continue working with it to form the top of the head.

HEAD

Rnd 1: While holding the second ear, take the first ear and continue single crocheting in each stitch around (18 sc); continue single crocheting in each stitch around of second ear (18 sc), making a total of 36 sc.
Rnd 2: *Sc5, 2sc in next*, repeat from * to * around. (42)
Rnd 3: *Sc6, 2sc in next*, repeat from * to * around. (48)
Rnd 4: *Sc7, 2sc in next*, repeat from * to * around. (54)
Rnd 5–Rnd 11: Sc1 in each stitch around. (54) You can cut the gray yarn.
Rnd 12–Rnd 14: With white sc1 in each stitch around. (54)
Rnd 15: *Sc7, sc2tog*, repeat from * to * around. (48)
Rnd 16: *Sc6, sc2tog*, repeat from * to * around. (42)

Rnd 17: *Sc5, sc2tog*, repeat from * to * around. (36)

Rnd 18: *Sc4, sc2tog*, repeat from * to * around. (30)

Rnd 19: *Sc3, sc2tog*, repeat from * to * around. (24)

Rnd 20: *Sc2, sc2tog*, repeat from * to * around. (18)

Take the safety eyes and attach them to the head between Rnd 9 and Rnd 10, and attach the safety nose between the eyes between Rnd 13 and Rnd 14. Now take a piece of gray yarn and sew across the top of the head to close off the ears so they won't be stuffed. Stuff the head. Cut the white yarn.

Rnd 21: *Sc1, sc2tog* repeat from * to * around. (12)

Cut a long tail and sew the seam closed.

Lastly, embroider three whiskers on each side of the nose, as shown in the picture.

BODY

Rnd 1: With gray ch18, 1dc in third ch from hook, dc14, 3dc in last, continue along other side of chains, dc15, 3dc in last, sl st in first dc. (36)

Rnd 2: Ch2 (doesn't count as first stitch now and throughout), dc3, **with white** dc11, **with gray** dc3, 2dc in next, dc17, 2dc in next, sl st in first dc. (38)

Rnd 3: With gray ch2, dc3, **with white** dc12, **with gray** dc3, 2dc in next, dc18, 2dc in next, sl st in first dc. (40)

Rnd 4: With gray ch2, dc3, **with white** dc13, **with gray** dc3, 2dc in next, dc19, 2dc in next, sl st in first dc. (42)

Rnd 5: With gray ch2, dc3, **with white** dc14, **with gray** dc3, 2dc in next, dc20, 2dc in next, sl st in first dc. (44)

Rnd 6: With gray ch2, dc3, **with white** dc15, **with gray** dc3, 2dc in next, dc21, 2dc in next, sl st in first dc. (46)

Rnd 7: With gray ch2, dc3, **with white** dc16, **with gray** dc3, 2dc in next, dc22, 2dc in next, sl st in first dc. (48)

Rnd 8: With gray ch2, dc3, **with white** dc17, **with gray** dc3, 2dc in next, dc23, 2dc in next, sl st in first dc. (50)

Rnd 9: With gray ch2, dc3, **with white** dc18, **with gray** dc3, 2dc in next, dc24, 2dc in next, sl st in first dc. (52)

Rnd 10: With gray ch2, dc3, **with white** dc19, **with gray** dc3, 2dc in next, dc25, 2dc in next, sl st in first dc. (54)

Rnd 11: With gray ch2, dc3, **with white** dc20, **with gray** dc3, 2dc in next, dc26, 2dc in next, sl st in first dc. (56)

Rnd 12: With gray ch2, dc3, **with white** dc21, with gray dc3, 2dc in next, dc27, 2dc in next, sl st in first dc. (58)

Rnd 13: With gray ch2, dc3, **with white** dc22, **with gray** dc3, 2dc in next, dc28, 2dc in next, sl st in first dc. (60)

Rnd 14: With gray ch2, dc3, **with white** dc23, **with gray** dc3, 2dc in next, dc29, 2dc in next, sl st in first dc. (62)

Rnd 15: With gray ch2, dc3, **with white** dc24, **with gray** dc3, 2dc in next, dc30, 2dc in next, sl st in first dc. (64)

Rnd 16: With gray ch2, dc3, **with white** dc25, **with gray** dc3, 2dc in next, dc31, 2dc in next, sl st in first dc. (66)

Rnd 17: With gray ch2, dc3, **with white** dc26, **with gray** dc3, 2dc in next, dc32, 2dc in next, sl st in first dc. (68)

Rnd 18: With gray ch2, dc3, **with white** dc27, **with gray** dc3, 2dc in next, dc33, 2dc in next, sl st in first dc. (70)

Rnd 19: With gray ch2, dc3, **with white** dc28, **with gray** dc3, 2dc in next, dc34, 2dc in next, sl st in first dc. (72)

Rnd 20: With gray ch2, dc3, **with white** dc29, **with gray** dc3, 2dc in next, dc35, 2dc in next, sl st in first dc. (74)

Cut a long tail to close the body in the end.

ARMS (MAKE 2)

Rnd 1: With white, start with a magic ring, 6sc in the loop. (6)
Rnd 2: 2sc in each stitch around. (12)
Rnd 3: *Sc1, 2sc in next*, repeat from * to * around. (18)
Rnd 4: *Sc2, 2sc in next*, repeat from * to * around. (24)
Rnd 5–Rnd 9: Sc in each stitch around. (24)
Rnd 10: *Sc2, sc2tog*, repeat from * to * around. (18)
Rnd 11–Rnd 12: Sc in each stitch around. (18)

Cut a long tail of the white yarn; you'll need it after Rnd 14.

Rnd 13: With gray sl st 1, ch2 (doesn't count as first stitch now and throughout), dc in each stitch around, sl st in first dc. (18)
Rnd 14: Ch2, dc2tog, dc in each stitch around, sl st in first dc. (17)

At this point, stuff the hand, take the yarn from Rnd 12, and sew across arm between Rnd 12 and Rnd 13.

Rnd 15: Ch2, dc in each stitch around, sl st in first dc. (17)
Rnd 16: Ch2, dc2tog, dc in each stitch around, sl st in first dc. (16)
Rnd 17: Ch2, dc in each stitch around, sl st in first dc. (16)
Rnd 18: Ch2, dc2tog, dc in each stitch around, sl st in first dc. (15)
Rnd 19: Ch2, dc in each stitch around, sl st in first dc. (15)
Rnd 20: Ch2, dc2tog, dc in each stitch around, sl st in first dc. (14)
Rnd 21: Ch2, dc in each stitch around, sl st in first dc. (14)
Rnd 22: Ch2, dc2tog, dc in each stitch around, sl st in first dc. (13)

Cut a long tail to attach arms to body later.

LEGS (MAKE 2)

Rnd 1: With white , start with a magic ring, ch2, 12dc in the loop, sl st in first dc. (12)

Rnd 2: Ch2, *dc1, 2dc in next*, repeat from * to * around, sl st in first dc. (18)

Rnd 3: Ch2, dc in each stitch around, sl st in first dc. (18)

Rnd 4–Rnd 7: With gray ch2, dc in each stitch around, sl st in first dc. (18)

Cut yarn and weave in ends.

PUTTING IT ALL TOGETHER

- Take the body and place both legs between the bottom two layers. Take the remaining yarn from the body and sew across the seam, with legs in between, to close and at the same time attach legs.
- Sew both arms to each side of the body between Rnd 2 and Rnd 4.
- Take the head and sew Rnd 15 of the head to Rnd 1 of the body.

BABY BUNNY

Kids love these little bunnies.

DIMENSIONS

5.5 in. (14 cm) long (not including ears) and 3.9 in. (10 cm) wide

MATERIALS

DK #3 lightweight yarn (sample shown in Scheepjes Stone Washed):
• pink (Red Jasper): 109.4 yd. (100 m)
• light pink (Rose Quartz): 65.6 yd. (60 m)
Crochet hook: US D-3 (3 mm)
Black safety eyes, 12 mm
Pink safety nose, 8 mm
Fiberfill stuffing
Yarn needle and scissors

DIFFICULTY LEVEL

EARS (MAKE 2)

Rnd 1: With pink, start with a magic ring, ch2, 6dc in the loop, sl st in first dc. (6)

Rnd 2: Ch2 (doesn't count as first dc), 2dc in each stitch around, sl st in first dc. (12)

Rnd 3: Ch2, *dc1, 2dc in next*, repeat from * to * around, sl st in first dc. (18)

Rnd 4–Rnd 5: Ch2, dc in each stitch around, sl st in first dc. (18)

Rnd 6: Ch2, *dc1, dc2tog*, repeat from * to * around, sl st in first dc. (12)

Rnd 7–Rnd 11: Ch2, dc1 in each stitch around, sl st in first dc. (12) Cut the yarn of the first ear, but don't cut the yarn of the second ear. You'll continue to work with it to make the top of the head.

HEAD

Rnd 1: With pink, while holding the second ear, take the first ear and single crochet in each stitch around (12), continue working sc1 in each stitch around of second ear (12), making a total of 24.

Rnd 2: *Sc3, 2sc in next*, repeat from * to * around. (30)

Rnd 3: *Sc4, 2sc in next*, repeat from * to * around. (36)

Rnd 4–Rnd 7: Sc1 in each stitch around. (36) You can cut the pink yarn.

Rnd 8–Rnd 9: With light pink sc1 in each stitch around. (36)

Rnd 10: * Sc4, sc2tog*, repeat from * to * around. (30)

Rnd 11: * Sc3, sc2tog*, repeat from * to * around. (24)

Rnd 12: * Sc2, sc2tog*, repeat from * to * around. (18)

Take the safety eyes and attach them to the head between Rnd 5 and Rnd 6 (ear not included) with 7 stitches in between, but make sure that the first stitches (where you see the color change) are on the back. Attach the safety nose between Rnd 8 and Rnd 9 and between the eyes. Now take a piece of pink yarn and sew across the top of the head to close off the ears so they won't be stuffed. Stuff the head.

Rnd 13: *Sc1, sc2tog*, repeat from * to * around. (12)

Cut a long tail and sew the seam closed.

BODY

Rnd 1: With pink ch13, dc1 in 3rd ch from hook, dc9, 3dc in last, continue along other side of chains, dc10, 3dc in last, sl st in first dc. (26)

Rnd 2: Ch2 (doesn't count as first stitch now and throughout), *dc12, 2dc in next* repeat from * to * one more time, sl st in first dc. (28)

Rnd 3: Ch2, dc3, **with light pink** dc7, **with pink** dc3, 2dc in next, dc13, 2dc in next, sl st in first dc. (30)

Rnd 4: Ch2, dc3, **with light pink** dc8, **with pink** dc3, 2dc in next, dc14, 2dc in next, sl st in first dc. (32)

Rnd 5: Ch2, dc3, **with light pink** dc9, **with pink** dc3, 2dc in next, dc15, 2dc in next, sl st in first dc. (34)

Rnd 6: Ch2, dc3, **with light pink** dc10, **with pink** dc3, 2dc in next, dc16, 2dc in next, sl st in first dc. (36)

Rnd 7: Ch2, dc3, **with light pink** dc11, **with pink** dc3, 2dc in next, dc17, 2dc in next, sl st in first dc. (38)

Rnd 8: Ch2, dc3, **with light pink** dc12, **with pink** dc3, 2dc in next, dc18, 2dc in next, sl st in first dc. (40)

Rnd 9: Ch2, dc3, **with light pink** dc13, **with pink** dc3, 2dc in next, dc19, 2dc in next, sl st in first dc. (42)

Rnd 10: Ch2, dc3, **with light pink** dc14, **with pink** dc3, 2dc in next, dc20, 2dc in next, sl st in first dc. (44)

Rnd 11: Ch2, dc3, **with light pink** dc15, **with pink** dc3, 2dc in next, dc21, 2dc in next, sl st in first dc. (46) Cut the light pink yarn and weave in the end.

Rnd 12: Ch2, *dc22, ch14, dc1 in 3rd ch from hook, dc1 in each of the remaining 11 chains, 2dc in next stitch of Rnd 11*, repeat from * to * one more time, sl st in first dc.

Cut a long tail to close the body later.

ARMS (MAKE 2)

Rnd 1: With pink, start with a magic ring, sc6 in the loop. (6)

Rnd 2: 2sc in each stitch around. (12)

Rnd 3: *Sc1, 2sc in next*, repeat from to * around. (18)

Rnd 4–Rnd 5: Sc1 in each stitch around. (18)

Rnd 6: *Sc1, sc2tog*, repeat from * to * around. (12)

Rnd 7: Sc1 in each stitch around. (12)

Rnd 8: Sl st 1, ch2 (doesn't count as first stitch now and throughout), dc1 in each stitch around, sl st in first dc. (12)

Rnd 9: Ch2, dc2tog, dc1 in each stitch around, sl st in first dc. (11)

At this point, stuff the hand and sew across arm between Rnd 7 and Rnd 8.

Rnd 10: Ch2, dc1 in each stitch around, sl st in first dc. (11)

Rnd 11: Ch2, dc2tog, dc1 in each stitch around, sl st in first dc. (10)

Rnd 12: Ch2, dc1 in each stitch around, sl st in first dc. (10)

Rnd 13: Ch2, dc2tog, dc1 in each stitch around, sl st in first dc. (9)

Cut a long tail to attach arms to body later.

PUTTING IT ALL TOGETHER

- Fold the body in line with the increases to make the belly straight and sew closed with the remaining yarn. Tie a knot in the corners to form the feet.
- Sew an arm to each side of the body in Rnd 1 and Rnd 2.
- Finally, take the head and sew Rnd 10 (ears not included) to Rnd 1 of the body.

CROCODILE

DIMENSIONS

11 in. (28 cm) high and 6.7 in. (17 cm) wide

MATERIALS

DK #3 lightweight yarn (sample shown in Scheepjes Stone Washed):
• green (Canada Jade): 284.3 yd. (260 m)
Crochet hook: US size D-3 (3 mm)
Brown and black safety eyes, 15 mm
Small amount of fiberfill stuffing
Yarn needle and scissors

DIFFICULTY LEVEL

EYES (MAKE 2)

Rnd 1: Start with a magic ring, 6sc in the loop. (6)
Rnd 2: 2sc in each stitch around. (12)
Rnd 3: *Sc1, 2sc in next*, repeat from * to * around. (18)
Rnd 4: *Sc2, 2sc in next*, repeat from * to * around. (24)
Rnd 5–Rnd 8: Sc1 in each stitch around. (24)

For the first eye, cut the yarn and secure the end. For the second eye, don't cut the yarn and continue with head instructions.

HEAD

The eyes will be connected to start the top of the head.
Rnd 1: Take both eyes, continue with second eye, sc11, take first eye and sc next stitch of second eye and first stitch of first eye together, sc22, sc next stitch of first eye and next stitch of second eye together, sc11. (46)
Rnd 2: Sc1 in each stitch around. (46)
Rnd 3: 2sc in first stitch, sc23, 2sc in next stitch, sc21. (48)
Rnd 4: 2sc in each of first 2 stitches, sc23, 2sc in each of next 2 stitches, sc21. (52)
Rnd 5: 2sc in each of first 4 stitches, sc23, 2sc in each of next 4 stitches, sc21. (60)
Rnd 6–Rnd 7: Sc1 in each stitch around. (60)
Rnd 8: Sc4, sc2tog, sc28, sc2tog, sc24. (58)
Rnd 9: Sc4, sc2tog, sc27, sc2tog, sc23. (56)
Rnd 10: Sc4, sc2tog, sc26, sc2tog, sc22. (54)
Rnd 11: Sc4, sc2tog, sc25, sc2tog, sc21. (52)
Rnd 12: Sc4, sc2tog, sc24, sc2tog, sc20. (50)
Rnd 13: Sc4, sc2tog, sc23, sc2tog, sc19. (48)
Rnd 14: Sc4, sc2tog, sc22, sc2tog, sc18. (46)
Rnd 15: Sc4, sc2tog, sc21, sc2tog, sc17. (44)
Rnd 16: Sc4, sc2tog, sc20, sc2tog, sc16. (42)
Rnd 17: Sc4, sc2tog, sc19, sc2tog, sc15. (40)
Rnd 18: Sc4, sc2tog, sc18, sc2tog, sc14. (38)
Rnd 19: Sc4, sc2tog, sc17, sc2tog, sc13. (36)
Rnd 20: Sc4, sc2tog, sc16, sc2tog, sc12. (34)
Rnd 21: Sc4, sc2tog, sc15, sc2tog, sc11. (32)
Rnd 22: Sc4, sc2tog, sc14, sc2tog, sc10. (30)
Rnd 23: Sc1 in each stitch around. (30)
Rnd 24: Sc3, sc2tog, sc13, sc2tog, sc10. (28)
Rnd 25: Sc1 in each stitch around. (28)

Rnd 26: Sc4, hdc1, dc3, hdc1, sc1, sl st1, sc1, hdc1, dc3, hdc1, sc1, hdc1, dc3, hdc1, sc1, sl st1, sc1, hdc1, dc1. (28)

Rnd 27: Dc2, hdc1, sc1, hdc1, dc3, hdc1, sc1, sl st1, sc1, hdc1, dc3, hdc1, sc1, hdc1, dc3, hdc1, sc1, sl st1, sc1, hdc1, dc1. (28)

Rnd 28: Dc2, hdc1, sc1, sl st 1. This is where this rnd ends. Cut a long tail. Now attach a safety eye to each side between Rnd 8 of the eyes and Rnd 1 of the head; stuff the head and sew the seam for the mouth closed.

BODY

Rnd 1: Ch20, dc in third ch from hook, dc16, 3dc in last, continue along other side of chains, dc17, 3dc in last, sl st in first dc. (40)

Rnd 2: Ch2 (doesn't count as first stitch now and throughout), *dc19, 2dc in next*, repeat from * to * one more time, sl st in first dc. (42)

Rnd 3: Ch2, *dc20, 2dc in next*, repeat from * to * one more time, sl st in first dc. (44)

Rnd 4: Ch2, *dc21, 2dc in next*, repeat from * to * one more time, sl st in first dc. (46)

Rnd 5: Ch2, *dc22, 2dc in next*, repeat from * to * one more time, sl st in first dc. (48)

Rnd 6: Ch2, *dc23, 2dc in next*, repeat from * to * one more time, sl st in first dc. (50)

Rnd 7: Ch2, *dc24, 2dc in next*, repeat from * to * one more time, sl st in first dc. (52)

Rnd 8: Ch2, *dc25, 2dc in next*, repeat from * to * one more time, sl st in first dc. (54)

Rnd 9: Ch2, *dc26, 2dc in next*, repeat from * to * one more time, sl st in first dc. (56)

Rnd 10: Ch2, *dc27, 2dc in next*, repeat from * to * one more time, sl st in first dc. (58)

Rnd 11: Ch2, *dc28, 2dc in next*, repeat from * to * one more time, sl st in first dc. (60)

Rnd 12: Ch2, *dc29, 2dc in next*, repeat from * to * one more time, sl st in first dc. (62)

Rnd 13: Ch2, *dc30, 2dc in next*, repeat from * to * one more time, sl st in first dc. (64)

Rnd 14: Ch2, *dc31, 2dc in next*, repeat from * to * one more time, sl st in first dc. (66)

Rnd 15: Ch2, *dc32, 2dc in next*, repeat from * to * one more time, sl st in first dc. (68)

Rnd 16: Ch2, *dc33, 2dc in next*, repeat from * to * one more time, sl st in first dc. (70)

Rnd 17: Ch2, *dc34, 2dc in next*, repeat from * to * one more time, sl st in first dc. (72)

Rnd 18: Ch2, *dc35, 2dc in next*, repeat from * to * one more time, sl st in first dc. (74)

Rnd 19: Ch2, *dc36, 2dc in next*, repeat from * to * one more time, sl st in first dc. (76)

Rnd 20: Ch2, *dc37, 2dc in next*, repeat from * to * one more time, sl st in first dc. (78)

Cut a long tail to close body and attach feet in the end.

FEET (MAKE 2)

Rnd 1: Start with a magic ring, 6sc in the loop. (6)

Rnd 2: 2sc in each stitch around. (12)

Rnd 3: *Sc1, 2sc in next*, repeat from * to * around. (18)

Rnd 4: *Sc2, 2sc in next*, repeat from * to * around. (24)

Rnd 5–Rnd 11: Sc1 in each stitch around. (24)

Rnd 12: *Sc1, (in next: hdc1, dc1, tr1, dc1, hdc1), sc1, sl st 1*, repeat from * to * around. You'll end up with three toes (6 repeats).

Cut a long tail to close the seam of the feet in the end.

TAIL

Rnd 1: Start with a magic ring, ch2 (doesn't count as first stitch from now on), 12dc in the loop, sl st in first dc. (12)

Rnd 2: Ch2, 2dc in each stitch around, sl st in first dc. (24)

Rnd 3: Ch2, dc5, 5dc in next, dc8, 5dc in next, dc8, 5dc in next, sl st in first dc. (36)

Rnd 4: Ch2, dc7, 5dc in next, dc12, 5dc in next, dc12, 5dc in next, dc2, sl st in first dc. (48)

Rnd 5: Ch2, dc9, 5dc in next, dc16, 5dc in next, dc16, 5dc in next, dc4, sl st in first dc. (60)

Rnd 6: Ch2, dc11, 3sc in next, *sc1, (in next: hdc1, dc1, tr1, dc1, hdc1), sc1, sl st 1*, repeat from * to * 4 more times, (in next: hdc1, dc1, tr1, dc1, hdc1), *sl st 1, sc1, (in next: hdc1, dc1, tr1, dc1, hdc1), sc1*, repeat from * to * 4 more times, 3sc in next, dc6, sl st in first dc.

Cut a long tail to close and attach to body in the end.

ARMS (MAKE 2)

Rnd 1: Start with a magic ring, 6sc in the loop. (6)

Rnd 2: 2sc in each stitch around. (12)

Rnd 3: *Sc1, 2sc in next*, repeat from * to * around. (18)

Rnd 4: *Sc2, 2sc in next*, repeat from * to * around. (24)

Rnd 5–Rnd 9: Sc1 in each stitch around. (24)

Rnd 10: *Sc2, sc2tog*, repeat from * to * around. (18)

Rnd 11–Rnd 12: Sc1 in each stitch around. (18)

Rnd 13: Sl st 1, ch2, dc1 in each stitch around, sl st in first dc. (18)

Rnd 14: Ch2, dc1 in each stitch around, sl st in first dc. (18) At this point, stuff the hand (not too much) and sew across the arm between Rnd 12 and Rnd 13.

Rnd 15–Rnd 17: Ch2, dc1 in each stitch around, sl st in first dc. (18)

Rnd 18: Ch2, *dc1, dc2tog*, repeat from * to * around, sl st in first dc. (12)

Rnd 19–Rnd 22: Ch2, dc1 in each stitch around, sl st in first dc. (12)

Cut a long tail to attach arms to body in the end.

PUTTING IT ALL TOGETHER

- Place each foot between the bottom two layers of the body; use the remaining yarn from the body and sew across the seam, with the feet in between, to close and at the same time attach the feet.

- Stuff the feet lightly. With the remaining yarn sew each foot closed, going through both layers of toes.
- Fold the tail in half so the spikes are lined up; sew closed. Sew the tail to the body.
- Sew the head to the top of the body.
- Finally, sew an arm to each side of the body.

BABY
CROCODILE

This freshly hatched baby croc needs a hug.

DIMENSIONS

7.1 in. (18 cm) long and 3.9 in. (10 cm) wide

MATERIALS

DK #3 lightweight yarn (sample shown in Scheepjes Stone Washed):
• green (819 New Jade): 142.2 yd. (130 m)
Crochet hook: US D-3 (3 mm)
Black safety eyes, 10 mm
Fiberfill stuffing
Yarn needle and scissors

Difficulty Level

EYES (MAKE 2)

Rnd 1: Start with a magic ring, 6sc in the loop. (6)
Rnd 2: 2sc in each stitch around. (12)
Rnd 3–Rnd 5: Sc1 in each stitch around. (12)
Cut yarn and weave in ends for the first eye; don't cut yarn for the second eye, but continue with instructions for the head.

HEAD

In the next rounds you'll connect the eyes to make the top of the head.
Rnd 1: Continue with the second eye, sc5, take the first eye and sc2tog in the next stitch of the second and first eyes through both layers. Sc10, sc2tog in the next stitch of the first and second eyes through both layers, sc5. (22)

Rnd 2: *2sc in first stitch, sc10*, repeat from * to * one more time. (24)

Rnd 3: *2sc in each of the next 2 stitches, sc10*, repeat from * to * one more time. (28)

Rnd 4: *2sc in each of the next 4 stitches, sc10*, repeat from * to * one more time. (36)

Rnd 5: Sc1 in each stitch around. (36)

Rnd 6: Sc4, sc2tog, sc16, sc2tog, sc12. (34)

Rnd 7: Sc4, sc2tog, sc15, sc2tog, sc11. (32)

Rnd 8: Sc4, sc2tog, sc14, sc2tog, sc10. (30) Attach safety eyes and center them in between Rnd 5 of the eyes and Rnd 1 of the head.

Rnd 9: Sc4, sc2tog, sc13, sc2tog, sc9. (28)

Rnd 10: Sc4, sc2tog, sc12, sc2tog, sc8. (26)

Rnd 11: Sc4, sc2tog, sc11, sc2tog, sc7. (24)

Rnd 12: Sc4, sc2tog, sc10, sc2tog, sc6. (22)

Rnd 13: Sc4, sc2tog, sc9, sc2tog, sc5. (20)

Rnd 14: Sc4, sc2tog, sc8, sc2tog, sc4. (18) Stuff the head.

Rnd 15: 4dc in next, sc3, 4dc in next, sc2, sl st1, sc2, 4dc in next, sc3, 4dc in next, sc1, sl st1. This round ends here. Cut a long tail, stuff the head more if needed, and sew the mouth shut.

BODY

Rnd 1: Ch13, 1dc in third ch from hook, dc9, 3dc in last, continue along other side of chains, dc10, 3dc in last, sl st in first dc. (26)

Rnd 2: Ch2 (doesn't count as first stitch now and throughout), *dc12, 2dc in next*, repeat from * to * one more time, sl st in first dc. (28)

Rnd 3: Ch2, *dc13, 2dc in next*, repeat from * to * one more time, sl st in first dc. (30)

Rnd 4: Ch2, *dc14, 2dc in next*, repeat from * to * one more time, sl st in first dc. (32)

Rnd 5: Ch2, *dc15, 2dc in next*, repeat from * to * one more time, sl st in first dc. (34)

Rnd 6: Ch2, *dc16, 2dc in next*, repeat from * to * one more time, sl st in first dc. (36)

Rnd 7: Ch2, *dc17, 2dc in next*, repeat from * to * one more time, sl st in first dc. (38)

Rnd 8: Ch2, *dc18, 2dc in next*, repeat from * to * one more time, sl st in first dc. (40)

Rnd 9: Ch2, *dc19, 2dc in next*, repeat from * to * one more time, sl st in first dc. (42)

Rnd 10: Ch2, *dc20, 2dc in next*, repeat from * to * one more time, sl st in first dc. (44)

Rnd 11: Ch2, *dc21, 2dc in next*, repeat from * to * one more time, sl st in first dc. (46)

Rnd 12: Ch2, *dc22, 2dc in next*, repeat from * to * one more time, sl st in first dc. (48)

Cut a long tail to close the body later.

ARMS (MAKE 2)

Rnd 1: Start with a magic ring, 6sc in the loop. (6)

Rnd 2: 2sc in each stitch around. (12)

Rnd 3: *Sc1, 2sc in next*, repeat from * to * around. (18)

Rnd 4–Rnd 5: Sc1 in each stitch around. (18)

Rnd 6: *Sc1, sc2tog*, repeat from * to * around. (12)

Rnd 7: Sc1 in each stitch around. (12)

Rnd 8: Sl st 1, ch2 (doesn't count as first stitch now and throughout), dc1 in each stitch around, sl st in first dc. (12)

Rnd 9: Ch2, dc2tog, dc1 in each stitch around, sl st in first dc. (11)

At this point, stuff the hand. Use a small piece of yarn and sew across the arm between Rnd 7 and Rnd 8.

Rnd 10: Ch2, dc1 in each stitch around, sl st in first dc. (11)

Rnd 11: Ch2, dc2tog, dc1 in each stitch around, sl st in first dc. (10)

Rnd 12: Ch2, dc1 in each stitch around, sl st in first dc. (10)

Cut a long tail to sew an arm to each side of the body between Rnd 1 and Rnd 3.

FEET (MAKE 2)

Rnd 1: Start with a magic ring, 6sc in the loop. (6)

Rnd 2: 2sc in each stitch around. (12)

Rnd 3: *Sc1, 2sc in next*, repeat from * to * around. (18)

Rnd 4–Rnd 5: Sc1 in each stitch around. (18)

Rnd 6: *Sc1, (in next: hdc1, dc1, tr1, dc1, hdc1), sl st 1*, repeat from * to * around. You'll end up with three toes (6 repeats).

Cut a long tail to close the feet at the end.

TAIL

Rnd 1: Start with a magic ring, ch2 (doesn't count as first dc for entire tail), dc12 in the loop, sl st in first dc. (12)

Rnd 2: Ch2, dc1, 5dc in next, dc4, 5dc in next, dc4, 5dc in next, sl st in first dc. (24)

Rnd 3: Ch2, dc3, 5dc in next, dc8, 5dc in next, dc8, 5dc in next, dc2, sl st in first dc. (36)

Rnd 4: Ch1 (doesn't count as first sc), sc5, 3sc in next, *sc1, 4dc in next, sc1*, repeat from * to * 3 more times, 3sc in next, *sc1, 4dc in next, sc1*, repeat from * to * 3 more times, 3sc in next, sc4, sl st in first sc. (72; you'll have one straight side and two sides with a pointy edging)

Cut a long tail to close the tail and sew it to the body at the end.

PUTTING IT ALL TOGETHER

- Place the feet in between the two layers of the body at the bottom. With the remaining yarn of the body, sew along the bottom to close the body and attach the feet at the same time.
- Stuff the feet lightly. With the remaining yarn, close each foot through both layers of the toes.
- Sew Rnd 5 of the head (eyes not included) to Rnd 1 of the body.
- Sew an arm to each side of the body in Rnds 1–3.
- Finally, fold the tail so the pointy edging is aligned and sew closed. Sew to one side of the body in the bottom 3 rounds.

DOG

This dog will be your loyal companion.

DIMENSIONS

12.2 in. (31 cm) long and 6.3 in. (16 cm) wide

MATERIALS

DK #3 lightweight yarn (sample shown in Scheepjes Stone Washed):
• ochre yellow (Yellow Jasper): 284.3 yd. (260 m)
Crochet hook: US size D-3 (3 mm)
Black and blue safety eyes, 15 mm
Black or brown safety nose, 15 mm
Fiberfill stuffing
Yarn needle and scissors

DIFFICULTY LEVEL

EYELIDS (MAKE 2)

Rnd 1: Start with a magic ring. 6sc in the ring. (6) When pulling the magic ring, put your hook inside to make sure you have enough room to put the safety eyes in later.
Rnd 2: Sl st 1, ch2 (doesn't count as first dc), dc4, ch1, sl st 1 in next. Cut yarn and weave in ends.

HEAD

Rnd 1: Start with a magic ring, 6sc in the ring. (6)
Rnd 2: 2sc in each stitch around. (12)
Rnd 3: *Sc1, 2sc in next*, repeat from * to * around. (18)

Rnd 4: *Sc2, 2sc in next*, repeat from * to * around. (24)

Rnd 5: *Sc3, 2sc in next*, repeat from * to * around. (30)

Rnd 6: *Sc4, 2sc in next*, repeat from * to * around. (36)

Rnd 7: *Sc5, 2sc in next*, repeat from * to * around. (42)

Rnd 8: *Sc6, 2sc in next*, repeat from * to * around. (48)

Rnd 9–Rnd 15: Sc1 in each stitch around. (48)

Rnd 16: 3sc in next, sc1, 3sc in next, sc45. (52)

Rnd 17: Sc1, 3sc in next, sc3, 3sc in next, sc46. (56)

Rnd 18: Sc2, 3sc in next, sc5, 3sc in next, sc47. (60)

Rnd 19: Sc3, 3sc in next, sc7, 3sc in next, sc48. (64)

Rnd 20–Rnd 24: Sc1 in each stitch around. (64)

Rnd 25: Sc7, sc5tog, sc52. (60)

Rnd 26: *Sc8, sc2tog*, repeat from * to * around. (54)

Rnd 27: *Sc7, sc2tog*, repeat from * to * around. (48)

Rnd 28: *Sc6, sc2tog*, repeat from * to * around. (42)

Rnd 29: *Sc5, sc2tog*, repeat from * to * around. (36)

Put a safety eye inside each eyelid. The eyelids will be folded over the top of the eyes. I recommend stuffing the head lightly to decide the placing of the eyes and nose. Now attach the eyes between Rnd 15 and Rnd 16 on each side of the snout (with 7 stitches in between) and make sure they are really secure, for safety reasons, since it is a little bit harder to attach them with two layers between the eye and the back.

Attach the safety nose between Rnd 21 and Rnd 22 in the center of the snout.

Rnd 30: *Sc4, sc2tog*, repeat from * to * around. (30)

Rnd 31: *Sc3, sc2tog*, repeat from * to * around. (24)

Rnd 32: *Sc2, sc2tog*, repeat from * to * around. (18) Stuff the head; make sure to stuff the snout to shape it.

Rnd 33: *Sc1, sc2tog*, repeat from * to * around. (12) Cut yarn, weave through the twelve remaining stitches, pull tight, and secure, leaving a long tail to attach it to the body later.

EARS (MAKE 2)

Rnd 1: Start with a magic ring, ch2 (doesn't count as first dc), dc12 in the loop, sl st in first dc. (12)

Rnd 2: Ch2, 2dc in each stitch around, sl st in first dc. (24)

Rnd 3–Rnd 4: Ch2, dc1 in each stitch around, sl st in first dc. (24)

Rnd 5: Ch2, *dc1, dc2tog*, repeat from * to * around, sl st in first dc. (16)

Rnd 6: Ch2, *dc6, dc2tog*, repeat from * to * around, sl st in first dc. (14)

Rnd 7: Ch2, *dc5, dc2tog *, repeat from * to * around, sl st in first dc. (12)

Rnd 8: Ch2, *dc4, dc2tog *, repeat from * to * around, sl st in first dc. (10)
Rnd 9: Ch2, *dc3, dc2tog *, repeat from * to * around, sl st in first dc. (8)
Rnd 10: Ch2, *dc2, dc2tog *, repeat from * to * around, sl st in first dc. (6)
Cut a long tail to attach ears to head later.

BODY

Rnd 1: Ch18, 1dc in third ch from hook, dc14, 3dc in last, continue along other side of chains, dc15, 3dc in last, sl st in first dc. (36)
Rnd 2: Ch2 (doesn't count as first stitch now and throughout), *dc17, 2dc in next*, repeat from * to * one more time, sl st in first dc. (38)
Rnd 3: Ch2, *dc18, 2dc in next*, repeat from * to * one more time, sl st in first dc. (40)
Rnd 4: Ch2, *dc19, 2dc in next*, repeat from * to * one more time, sl st in first dc. (42)
Rnd 5: Ch2, *dc20, 2dc in next*, repeat from * to * one more time, sl st in first dc. (44)
Rnd 6: Ch2, *dc21, 2dc in next*, repeat from * to * one more time, sl st in first dc. (46)
Rnd 7: Ch2, *dc22, 2dc in next*, repeat from * to * one more time, sl st in first dc. (48)
Rnd 8: Ch2, *dc23, 2dc in next*, repeat from * to * one more time, sl st in first dc. (50)
Rnd 9: Ch2, *dc24, 2dc in next*, repeat from * to * one more time, sl st in first dc. (52)
Rnd 10: Ch2, *dc25, 2dc in next*, repeat from * to * one more time, sl st in first dc. (54)
Rnd 11: Ch2, *dc26, 2dc in next*, repeat from * to * one more time, sl st in first dc. (56)
Rnd 12: Ch2, *dc27, 2dc in next*, repeat from * to * one more time, sl st in first dc. (58)
Rnd 13: Ch2, *dc28, 2dc in next*, repeat from * to * one more time, sl st in first dc. (60)
Rnd 14: Ch2, *dc29, 2dc in next*, repeat from * to * one more time, sl st in first dc. (62)
Rnd 15: Ch2, *dc30, 2dc in next*, repeat from * to * one more time, sl st in first dc. (64)
Rnd 16: Ch2, *dc31, 2dc in next*, repeat from * to * one more time, sl st in first dc. (66)
Rnd 17: Ch2, *dc32, 2dc in next*, repeat from * to * one more time, sl st in first dc. (68)

Rnd 18: Ch2, *dc33, 2dc in next*, repeat from * to * one more time, sl st in first dc. (70)

Rnd 19: Ch2, *dc34, 2dc in next*, repeat from * to * one more time, sl st in first dc. (72)

Rnd 20: Ch2, *dc35, 2dc in next*, repeat from * to * one more time, sl st in first dc. (74)

Cut a long tail to close the body; fold the body in line with the increases to make the belly straight.

LEGS (MAKE 2)

Rnd 1: Start with a magic ring, ch2 (doesn't count as first dc), dc12 in the loop, sl st in first dc. (12)

Rnd 2: Ch2, *dc1, 2dc in next*, repeat from * to * around, sl st in first dc. (18)

Rnd 3–Rnd 7: Ch2, dc1 in each stitch around, sl st in first dc. (18) Cut yarn and weave in ends.

TAIL

Rnd 1: Start with a magic ring, ch2 (doesn't count as first dc), dc12 in the loop, sl st in first dc. (12)

Rnd 2–Rnd 4: Ch2, dc1 in each stitch around, sl st in first dc. (12)

Cut yarn and weave in ends.

ARMS (MAKE 2)

Rnd 1: Start with a magic ring, 6sc in the loop. (6)

Rnd 2: 2sc in each stitch around. (12)

Rnd 3: *Sc1, 2sc in next*, repeat from * to * around. (18)

Rnd 4: *Sc2, 2sc in next*, repeat from * to * around. (24)

Rnd 5–Rnd 9: Sc1 in each stitch around. (24)

Rnd 10: *Sc2, sc2tog*, repeat from * to * around. (18)

Rnd 11–Rnd 12: Sc1 in each stitch around. (18)

Rnd 13: Sl st 1, ch2 (doesn't count as first stitch now and throughout), dc1 in each stitch around, sl st in first dc. (18)

Rnd 14: Ch2, dc2tog, dc1 in each stitch around, sl st in first dc. (17)

At this point, stuff the hand. Take a small piece of the yarn and sew across the arm between Rnd 12 and Rnd 13.

Rnd 15: Ch2, dc1 in each stitch around, sl st in first dc. (17)

Rnd 16: Ch2, dc2tog, dc1 in each stitch around, sl st in first dc. (16)

Rnd 17: Ch2, dc1 in each stitch around, sl st in first dc. (16)

Rnd 18: Ch2, dc2tog, dc1 in each stitch around, sl st in first dc. (15)

Rnd 19: Ch2, dc1 in each stitch around, sl st in first dc. (15)
Rnd 20: Ch2, dc2tog, dc1 in each stitch around, sl st in first dc. (14)
Rnd 21: Ch2, dc1 in each stitch around, sl st in first dc. (14)
Rnd 22: Ch2, dc2tog, dc1 in each stitch around, sl st in first dc. (13)
Cut a long tail to attach arms to body later.

PUTTING IT ALL TOGETHER

- Sew ears to each side of the head in Rnd 10.
- Place both legs and the tail between the bottom two layers of the body. With the remaining yarn from the body, sew across the seam with the parts in between. This way you close the bottom and assemble the pieces at the same time.
- Sew an arm to each side of the body between Rnd 1 and Rnd 3.
- Finally, sew Rnd 27 of the head to Rnd 1 of the body.

PUPPY

DIMENSIONS

6.3 in (16 cm) long and 3.9 in (10 cm) wide

MATERIALS

DK #3 lightweight yarn (sample shown in Scheepjes Stone Washed):
• brown (Brown Agate): 142.2 yd. (130 m)
Crochet hook: US size D-3 (3 mm)
Black and blue safety eyes, 15 mm
Black or brown safety nose, 15 mm
Fiberfill stuffing
Yarn needle and scissors

DIFFICULTY LEVEL

EYELIDS (MAKE 2)

Rnd 1: Start with a magic ring, 6sc in the ring. (6) When pulling the magic ring, put your hook inside to make sure you have enough room to put the safety eye in later.
Rnd 2: *Sc1, 2sc in next*, repeat from * to * one more time, sl st 1 to finish. Cut yarn and weave in ends.

HEAD

Rnd 1: Start with a magic ring, 6sc in the ring. (6)
Rnd 2: 2sc in each stitch around. (12)
Rnd 3: *Sc1, 2sc in next*, repeat from * to * around. (18)
Rnd 4: *Sc2, 2sc in next*, repeat from * to * around. (24)
Rnd 5: *Sc3, 2sc in next*, repeat from * to * around. (30)
Rnd 6: *Sc4, 2sc in next*, repeat from * to * around. (36)

Rnd 7–Rnd 11: Sc1 in each stitch around. (36)

Rnd 12: 2sc in each of the next 5 stitches (this will be the snout), sc31. (41)

Rnd 13–Rnd 16: Sc1 in each stitch around. (41)

Rnd 17: Sc2tog 5 times, sc31. (36)

Rnd 18: *Sc4, sc2tog*, repeat from * to * around. (30)

Rnd 19: *Sc3, sc2tog*, repeat from * to * around. (24)

Rnd 20: *Sc2, sc2tog*, repeat from * to * around. (18)

Put a safety eye inside each eyelid; the eyelids will be folded over the top of the eyes. Now attach the eyes between Rnd 10 and Rnd 11 on each side of the snout and make sure they are really secure, for safety reasons, since it is a little bit harder to attach them with two layers between the eye and the back.

Attach the safety nose between Rnd 13 and Rnd 14 in the center of the snout and stuff the head; make sure to stuff the snout to shape it.

Rnd 21: *Sc1, sc2tog*, repeat from * to * around. (12) Cut yarn, weave through the twelve remaining stitches, pull tight, and secure, but leave a long tail to attach it to the body later.

EARS (MAKE 2)

Rnd 1: Start with a magic ring, 6sc in the ring. (6)

Rnd 2: 2sc in each stitch around. (12)

Rnd 3–Rnd 4: Sc1 in each stitch around. (12)

Rnd 5: *Sc1, sc2tog*, repeat from * to * around. (8)

Rnd 6–Rnd 9: Sc1 in each stitch around. (8) Cut yarn but leave a long tail to attach ears to head later.

BODY

Rnd 1: Ch13, 1dc in third ch from hook, dc9, 3dc in last, continue along other side of chains, dc9, 4dc in last, sl st in first dc. (26)

Rnd 2: Ch2 (doesn't count as first stitch now and throughout), *dc12, 2dc in next*, repeat from * to * one more time, sl st in first dc. (28)

Rnd 3: Ch2, *dc13, 2dc in next*, repeat from * to * one more time, sl st in first dc. (30)

Rnd 4: Ch2, *dc14, 2dc in next*, repeat from * to * one more time, sl st in first dc. (32)

Rnd 5: Ch2, *dc15, 2dc in next*, repeat from * to * one more time, sl st in first dc. (34)

Rnd 6: Ch2, *dc16, 2dc in next*, repeat from * to * one more time, sl st in first dc. (36)

Rnd 7: Ch2, *dc17, 2dc in next*, repeat from * to * one more time, sl st in first dc. (38)

Rnd 8: Ch2, *dc18, 2dc in next*, repeat from * to * one more time, sl st in first dc. (40)

Rnd 9: Ch2, *dc19, 2dc in next*, repeat from * to * one more time, sl st in first dc. (42)

Rnd 10: Ch2, *dc20, 2dc in next*, repeat from * to * one more time, sl st in first dc. (44)

Rnd 11: Ch2, *dc21, 2dc in next*, repeat from * to * one more time, sl st in first dc. (46)

Rnd 12: Ch2, *dc22, ch14, 1dc in third ch from hook, 1dc in each of the 11 remaining chains, 2dc in next stitch of Rnd 11*, repeat from * to * one more time, sl st in first dc. Cut a long tail to close the body.

ARMS (MAKE 2)

Rnd 1: Start with a magic ring, 6sc in the loop. (6)

Rnd 2: 2sc in each stitch around. (12)

Rnd 3: *Sc1, 2sc in next*, repeat from * to * around. (18)

Rnd 4–Rnd 5: Sc1 in each stitch around. (18)

Rnd 6: *Sc1, sc2tog*, repeat from * to * around. (12)

Rnd 7: Sc1 in each stitch around. (12)

Rnd 8: Sl st 1, ch2 (doesn't count as first stitch now and throughout), dc1 in each stitch around, sl st in first dc. (12)

Rnd 9: Ch2, dc2tog, dc1 in each stitch around, sl st in first dc. (11)

At this point, stuff the hand, take a small piece of the brown yarn, and sew across the arm between Rnd 7 and Rnd 8.

Rnd 10: Ch2, dc1 in each stitch around, sl st in first dc. (11)

Rnd 11: Ch2, dc2tog, dc1 in each stitch around, sl st in first dc. (10)

Rnd 12: Ch2, dc1 in each stitch around, sl st in first dc. (10)

Rnd 13: Ch2, dc2tog, dc1 in each stitch around, sl st in first dc. (9)

Cut a long tail to attach arms to body later.

PUTTING IT ALL TOGETHER

- Sew an ear on either side of the head at Rnd 6.
- Fold the body along the increase lines to make the belly straight and sew it closed. Tie a knot in the corners to form the feet.
- Sew an arm on either side of the body between Rnd 1 and Rnd 2.
- Sew Rnd 18 of the head to Rnd 1 of the body.

FOX

You will want to cuddle this very soft fox.

DIMENSIONS

10.6 in. (27 cm) long and 6.3 in. (16 cm) wide

MATERIALS

DK #3 lightweight yarn (sample shown in Scheepjes Stone Washed):
• orange (Coral): 142.2 yd. (130 m)
• white (Moon Stone): 76.6 yd. (70 m)
• black (Black Onyx): 76.6 yd. (70 m)
Crochet hook: US size D-3 (3 mm)
Black and gold safety eyes, 15 mm
Fiberfill stuffing
Yarn needle and scissors

DIFFICULTY LEVEL

HEAD

Rnd 1: With black, start with a magic ring, 6sc in the loop. (6)
Rnd 2: *Sc1, 2sc in next*, repeat from * to * around. (9)
Rnd 3: With white *Sc2, 2sc in next*, repeat from * to * around. (12)
Rnd 4: *Sc3, 2sc in next*, repeat from * to * around. (15)
Rnd 5: *Sc4, 2sc in next*, repeat from * to * around. (18)
Rnd 6: *Sc5, 2sc in next*, repeat from * to * around. (21)
Rnd 7: *Sc6, 2sc in next*, repeat from * to * around. (24)
Rnd 8: With orange *sc3, 2sc in next*, repeat from * to * around. (30)
Rnd 9: *Sc4, 2sc in next*, repeat from * to * around. (36)
Rnd 10: *Sc5, 2sc in next*, repeat from * to * around. (42)

Rnd 11: *Sc6, 2sc in next*, repeat from * to * around. (48)

Rnd 12–Rnd 21: Sc1 in each stitch around. (48)

Attach a safety eye between Rnd 12 and Rnd 13, on either side of the snout; make sure the first stitch (where you can see the color change) is on the back.

Rnd 22: *Sc6, sc2tog*, repeat from * to * around. (42)

Rnd 23: *Sc5, sc2tog*, repeat from * to * around. (36)

Rnd 24: *Sc4, sc2tog*, repeat from * to * around. (30)

Rnd 25: *Sc3, sc2tog*, repeat from * to * around. (24)

Rnd 26: *Sc2, sc2tog*, repeat from * to * around. (18)

Stuff the head.

Rnd 27: *Sc1, sc2tog*, repeat from * to * around. (12)

Cut a long thread, weave through the front loops of the remaining stitches, pull tight, secure, and weave in ends.

EARS (MAKE 2)

Rnd 1: With black, start with a magic ring, 6sc in the loop. (6)

Rnd 2: *Sc1, 2sc in next*, repeat from * to * around. (9)

Rnd 3: *Sc2, 2sc in next*, repeat from * to * around. (12)

Rnd 4: With orange *sc3, 2sc in next*, repeat from * to * around. (15)

Rnd 5: *Sc4, 2sc in next*, repeat from * to * around. (18)

Rnd 6: *Sc5, 2sc in next*, repeat from * to * around. (21)

Rnd 7–Rnd 10: Sc1 in each stitch around. (21)

Cut the yarn but leave a long tail to attach the ears in the end.

BODY

Rnd 1: With orange ch18, 1dc in third ch from hook, dc14, 3dc in last, continue along other side of chains, dc15, 3dc in last, sl st in first dc. (36)

Rnd 2: Ch2 (doesn't count as first stitch now and throughout), *dc17, 2dc in next*, repeat from * to * one more time, sl st in first dc. (38)

Rnd 3: Ch2, *dc18, 2dc in next*, repeat from * to * one more time, sl st in first dc. (40)

Rnd 4: Ch2, *dc19, 2dc in next*, repeat from * to * one more time, sl st in first dc. (42)

Rnd 5: Ch2, *dc20, 2dc in next*, repeat from * to * one more time, sl st in first dc. (44)

Rnd 6: Ch2, *dc21, 2dc in next*, repeat from * to * one more time, sl st in first dc. (46)

Rnd 7: Ch2, *dc22, 2dc in next*, repeat from * to * one more time, sl st in first dc. (48)

Rnd 8: Ch2, *dc23, 2dc in next*, repeat from * to * one more time, sl st in first dc. (50)

Rnd 9: Ch2, *dc24, 2dc in next*, repeat from * to * one more time, sl st in first dc. (52)

Rnd 10: Ch2, *dc25, 2dc in next*, repeat from * to * one more time, sl st in first dc. (54)

Rnd 11: Ch2, *dc26, 2dc in next*, repeat from * to * one more time, sl st in first dc. (56)

Rnd 12: Ch2, *dc27, 2dc in next*, repeat from * to * one more time, sl st in first dc. (58)

Rnd 13: Ch2, *dc28, 2dc in next*, repeat from * to * one more time, sl st in first dc. (60)

Rnd 14: Ch2, *dc29, 2dc in next*, repeat from * to * one more time, sl st in first dc. (62)

Rnd 15: Ch2, *dc30, 2dc in next*, repeat from * to * one more time, sl st in first dc. (64)

Rnd 16: Ch2, *dc31, 2dc in next*, repeat from * to * one more time, sl st in first dc. (66)

Rnd 17: Ch2, *dc32, 2dc in next*, repeat from * to * one more time, sl st in first dc. (68)

Rnd 18: Ch2, *dc33, 2dc in next*, repeat from * to * one more time, sl st in first dc. (70)

Rnd 19: Ch2, *dc34, 2dc in next*, repeat from * to * one more time, sl st in first dc. (72)

Cut a long tail to close the body; fold the body in line with the increases to make the belly straight.

ARMS (MAKE 2)

Rnd 1: With black, start with a magic ring, 6sc in the loop.(6)

Rnd 2: 2sc in each stitch around. (12)

Rnd 3: *Sc1, 2sc in next*, repeat from * to * around. (18)

Rnd 4: *Sc2, 2sc in next*, repeat from * to * around. (24)

Rnd 5–Rnd 9: Sc1 in each stitch around. (24)

Rnd 10: *Sc2, sc2tog*, repeat from * to * around. (18)

Rnd 11–Rnd 12: Sc1 in each stitch around. (18)

Cut a long thread; you'll use it after Rnd 14.

Rnd 13: With orange sl st 1, ch2 (doesn't count as first stitch now and throughout), dc1 in each stitch around, sl st in first dc. (18)

Rnd 14: Ch2, dc2tog, dc1 in each stitch around, sl st in first dc. (17)

At this point, stuff the hand. Take the remaining black yarn and sew across the arm between Rnd 12 and Rnd 13.

Rnd 15: Ch2, dc1 in each stitch around, sl st in first dc. (17)
Rnd 16: Ch2, dc2tog, dc1 in each stitch around, sl st in first dc. (16)
Rnd 17: Ch2, dc1 in each stitch around, sl st in first dc. (16)
Rnd 18: Ch2, dc2tog, dc1 in each stitch around, sl st in first dc. (15)
Rnd 19: Ch2, dc1 in each stitch around, sl st in first dc. (15)
Rnd 20: Ch2, dc2tog, dc1 in each stitch around, sl st in first dc. (14)
Rnd 21: Ch2, dc1 in each stitch around, sl st in first dc. (14)
Rnd 22: Ch2, dc2tog, dc1 in each stitch around, sl st in first dc. (13)
Cut a long tail to attach arms to body later.

LEGS (MAKE 2)

Rnd 1: With black, start with a magic ring, ch2 (doesn't count as first dc), 12dc in the loop, sl st in first dc. (12)
Rnd 2: Ch2, *dc1, 2dc in next*, repeat from * to * around, sl st in first dc. (18)
Rnd 3–Rnd 4: Ch2, dc1 in each stitch around, sl st in first dc. (18)
Rnd 5–Rnd 6: With orange ch2, dc1 in each stitch around, sl st in first dc. (18)
Cut yarn and weave in ends.

TAIL

Rnd 1: With white, start with a magic ring, ch2 (doesn't count as first dc), 6dc in the loop, sl st in first dc. (6)
Rnd 2: Ch2, *dc1, 2dc in next*, repeat from * to * around, sl st in first dc. (9)
Rnd 3: Ch2, *dc2, 2dc in next*, repeat from * to * around, sl st in first dc. (12)
Rnd 4: Ch2, *dc3, 2dc in next*, repeat from * to * around, sl st in first dc. (15)
Rnd 5: With orange ch2, *dc2, 2dc in next*, repeat from * to * around, sl st in first dc. (20)
Rnd 6: Ch2, *dc3, 2dc in next*, repeat from * to * around, sl st in first dc. (25)
Rnd 7: Ch2, *dc4, 2dc in next*, repeat from * to * around, sl st in first dc. (30)
Rnd 8–Rnd 9: Ch2, dc1 in each stitch around, sl st in first dc. (30)
Rnd 10: Ch2, *dc3, dc2tog*, repeat from * to * around, sl st in first dc. (24)
Rnd 11: Ch2, *dc2, dc2tog*, repeat from * to * around, sl st in first dc. (18)
Rnd 12: Ch2, *dc1, dc2tog*, repeat from * to * around, sl st in first dc. (12)
Cut a long tail to attach tail to body later.

PUTTING IT ALL TOGETHER

- Place the legs between the bottom two layers of the body. With the remaining yarn from the body, sew across the seam with the legs in between. This way you close the bottom and assemble the pieces at the same time.
- Sew the tail to the body against the bottom 3 rounds.
- Sew an arm to each side of the body between Rnd 1 and Rnd 3.
- Use pins to determine the placement of the ears. For example, attach them with a slight rounding, one corner from Rnd 22 and the other corner from Rnd 17; in Rnd 22 they are 6 stitches apart. Sew the ears in place.
- Finally, sew Rnd 16 of the head to Rnd 1 of the body.

KIT

You will never want to let go of this little fox!

DIMENSIONS

5.9 in. (15 cm) long and 3.9 in. (10 cm) wide

MATERIALS

DK #3 lightweight yarn (sample shown in Scheepjes Stone Washed):
• orange (Coral): 120.3 yd. (110 m)
• white (Moon Stone): 32.8 yd. (30 m)
• black (Black Onyx): 54.7 yd. (50 m)
Crochet hook: US size D-3 (3 mm)
Black with gold safety eyes, 12 mm
Fiberfill stuffing
Yarn needle and scissors

DIFFICULTY LEVEL

HEAD

Rnd 1: With black, start with a magic ring, 6sc in the loop. (6)
Rnd 2: *Sc1, 2sc in next*, repeat from * to * around. (9)
Rnd 3: With white *sc2, 2sc in next*, repeat from * to * around. (12)
Rnd 4: *Sc3, 2sc in next*, repeat from * to * around. (15)
Rnd 5: *Sc4, 2sc in next*, repeat from * to * around. (18)
Rnd 6: With orange *sc2, 2sc in next*, repeat from * to * around. (24)
Rnd 7: *Sc3, 2sc in next*, repeat from * to * around. (30)
Rnd 8: *Sc4, 2sc in next*, repeat from * to * around. (36)
Rnd 9–Rnd 16: Sc1 in each stitch around. (36)

Attach the safety eyes between Rnd 8 and Rnd 9, on both sides of the snout, but make sure that the first stitch (where you can see the color change) is on the back.

Rnd 17: *Sc4, sc2tog*, repeat from * to * around. (30)

Rnd 18: *Sc3, sc2tog*, repeat from * to * around. (24)

Rnd 19: *Sc2, sc2tog*, repeat from * to * around. (18) Stuff the head.

Rnd 20: *Sc1, sc2tog*, repeat from * to * around. (12)

Cut a long thread, weave through the front loops of the remaining stitches, pull tight, secure and weave in ends.

EARS (MAKE 2)

Rnd 1: With black, start with a magic ring, 6sc in the loop. (6)

Rnd 2: *Sc1, 2sc in next*, repeat from * to * around. (9)

Rnd 3: *Sc2, 2sc in next*, repeat from * to * around. (12)

Rnd 4: With orange *sc3, 2sc in next*, repeat from * to * around. (15)

Rnd 5–Rnd 7: Sc1 in each stitch around. (15)

Cut the yarn but leave a long tail to attach the ears in the end.

BODY

Rnd 1: With orange ch13, dc1 in 3rd ch from hook, dc9, 3dc in last, continue along other side of chains, dc10, 3dc in last, sl st in first dc. (26)

Rnd 2: Ch2 (doesn't count as first stitch now and throughout), *dc12, 2dc in next* repeat from * to * one more time, sl st in first dc. (28)

Rnd 3: Ch2, *dc13, 2dc in next*, repeat from * to * one more time, sl st in first dc. (30)

Rnd 4: Ch2, *dc14, 2dc in next*, repeat from * to * one more time, sl st in first dc. (32)

Rnd 5: Ch2, *dc15, 2dc in next*, repeat from * to * one more time, sl st in first dc. (34)

Rnd 6: Ch2, *dc16, 2dc in next*, repeat from * to * one more time, sl st in first dc. (36)

Rnd 7: Ch2, *dc17, 2dc in next*, repeat from * to * one more time, sl st in first dc. (38)

Rnd 8: Ch2, *dc18, 2dc in next*, repeat from * to * one more time, sl st in first dc. (40)

Rnd 9: Ch2, *dc19, 2dc in next*, repeat from * to * one more time, sl st in first dc. (42)

Rnd 10: Ch2, *dc20, 2dc in next*, repeat from * to * one more time, sl st in first dc. (44)

Rnd 11: Ch2, *dc21, 2dc in next*, repeat from * to * one more time, sl st in first dc. (46)

Rnd 12: Ch2, ***with orange** dc22, **with black** ch14, dc1 in 3rd ch from hook, dc1 in each of the remaining 11 chains, **with orange** 2dc in next stitch of Rnd 11*, repeat from * to * one more time, sl st in first dc. Cut a long tail to close the body later.

ARMS (MAKE 2)

Rnd 1: With black, start with a magic ring, 6sc in the loop. (6)

Rnd 2: 2sc in each stitch around. (12)

Rnd 3: *Sc1, 2sc in next*, repeat from * to * around. (18)

Rnd 4–Rnd 5: Sc1 in each stitch around. (18)

Rnd 6: *Sc1, sc2tog*, repeat from * to * around. (12)

Rnd 7: Sc1 in each stitch around. (12) Cut a long thread; you'll use it after Rnd 9.

Rnd 8: With orange sl st 1, ch2 (doesn't count as first stitch now and throughout), dc1 in each stitch around, sl st in first dc. (12)

Rnd 9: Ch2, dc2tog, dc1 in each stitch around, sl st in first dc. (11)

At this point, stuff the hand. Take the remaining black yarn and sew across the arm between Rnd 7 and Rnd 8.

Rnd 10: Ch2, dc1 in each stitch around, sl st in first dc. (11)

Rnd 11: Ch2, dc2tog, dc1 in each stitch around, sl st in first dc. (10)

Rnd 12: Ch2, dc1 in each stitch around, sl st in first dc. (10)

Rnd 13: Ch2, dc2tog, dc1 in each stitch around, sl st in first dc. (9)

Cut a long tail to attach arms to body later.

TAIL

Rnd 1: With white, start with a magic ring, ch2 (doesn't count as first dc), 6dc in the loop, sl st in first dc. (6)

Rnd 2: Ch2, *dc1, 2dc in next*, repeat from * to * around, sl st in first dc. (9)

Rnd 3: Ch2, *dc2, 2dc in next*, repeat from * to * around, sl st in first dc. (12)

Rnd 4: With orange ch2, *dc1, 2dc in next*, repeat from * to * around, sl st in first dc. (18)

Rnd 5: Ch2, *dc2, 2dc in next*, repeat from * to * around, sl st in first dc. (24)

Rnd 6: Ch2, dc1 in each stitch around, sl st in first dc. (24)

Rnd 7: Ch2, *dc2, dc2tog*, repeat from * to * around, sl st in first dc. (18)

Rnd 8: Ch2, *dc1, dc2tog*, repeat around, sl st in first dc. (12) Cut a long thread to attach tail to body later.

PUTTING IT ALL TOGETHER

- Use pins to determine the placement of the ears. Attach them with a slight rounding, the top corner in Rnd 16 of the head and the other corner in Rnd 12; at the top of the head, in Rnd 16, the ears are 6 stitches apart. Sew the ears in place.
- Fold the body in line with the increases to make the belly straight and sew closed with the remaining yarn. Tie a knot in the corners to form the feet.
- Sew an arm to each side of the body in Rnd 1 and Rnd 2.
- Sew the tail to the body against Rnd 10 to Rnd 12.
- Finally, sew Rnd 13 of the head to Rnd 1 of the body.

FROG

DIMENSIONS

14.2 in. (36 cm) high and 5.9 in. (15 cm) wide

MATERIALS

DK #3 lightweight yarn (sample shown in Scheepjes Stone Washed):
• light green (New Jade): 87.5 yd. (80 m)
• dark green (Canada Jade): 196.9 yd. (180 m)
Crochet hook: US size D-3 (3 mm)
Gold and black safety eyes, 15 mm
Fiberfill stuffing
Needle and scissors

DIFFICULTY LEVEL

EYES (MAKE 2)

Rnd 1: With dark green, start with a magic ring, 6sc in the ring. (6)
Rnd 2: 2sc in each stitch around. (12)
Rnd 3: *Sc1, 2sc in next*, repeat from * to * around. (18)
Rnd 4: *Sc2, 2sc in next*, repeat from * to * around. (24)
Rnd 5–Rnd 8: Sc1 in each stitch around. (24)
For the first eye, tie the thread off; for the second eye, let the thread hang and continue with the head.

HEAD

The eyes are connected and form the top of the head.
Rnd 1: Continue with the second eye, sc11, take the first eye and crochet the next stitch of the second eye and the first eye together, sc22, crochet the next stitch of the first and second eye together, sc11. (46)
Rnd 2: 2sc in first stitch, sc22, 2sc in next stitch, sc22. (48)
Rnd 3: *Sc7, 2sc in next*, repeat from * to * around. (54)
Rnd 4–Rnd 8: Sc1 in each stitch around. (54)
Rnd 9: With dark green sc7, **with light green** sc18, **with dark green** sc29. (54)
Rnd 10: With dark green sc8, **with light green** sc17, **with dark green** sc29. (54)

Rnd 11: With dark green sc9, **with light green** sc16, **with dark green** sc29. (54)

Rnd 12: With dark green sc10, **with light green** sc15, **with dark green** sc29. (54)

Rnd 13: With dark green sc7, sc2tog, sc2, **with light green** sc5, sc2tog, sc5, sc2tog, **with dark green** sc9, *sc2tog, sc7*, repeat from * to * to last 2 stitches, sc2tog. (48)

Rnd 14: With dark green sc6, sc2tog, sc3, **with light green** sc4, sc2tog, sc3, sc2tog, **with dark green** *sc6, sc2tog*, repeat from * to * to last 2 stitches, sc2. (42)

Rnd 15: With dark green sc5, sc2tog, sc4, **with light green** sc1, sc2tog, sc3, sc2tog, **with dark green** sc7, *sc2tog, sc5*, repeat from * to * to last 2 stitches, sc2tog. (36)

Rnd 16: With dark green sc4, sc2tog, sc3, sc2tog, **with light green** sc3, sc2tog, **with dark green** *sc4, sc2tog*, repeat from * to * until last 2 stitches, sc2. (30)

Rnd 17: With dark green sc3, sc2tog, sc3, sc2tog, **with light green** sc3, **with dark green** sc2tog, *sc3, sc2tog*, repeat from * to * to end. (24)

Rnd 18: With dark green sc2, sc2tog, sc2, sc2tog, sc1, **with light green** sc2tog, **with dark green** *sc2, sc2tog*, repeat from * to * to last stitch, sc1. (18) You can cut the light green thread.

At this point, attach the eyes between Rnd 8 of the eye and Rnd 1 of the head and fill the head.

Rnd 19: With dark green *sc1, sc2tog*, repeat from * to * around. (12)

Cut the thread, close the seam with the dark green thread, and neatly hide the light green thread.

BODY

Rnd 1: With dark green ch18, dc1 in third ch from crochet hook, dc14, 3dc in last, continue to crochet along other side of chains, dc15, 3dc in last, sl st in first dc. (36)

Rnd 2: Ch2 (does not count as first st for the entire pattern), dc3, **with light green** dc11, **with dark green** dc3, 2dc in next, dc17, 2dc in next, sl st in first dc. (38)

Rnd 3: With dark green ch2, dc3, **with light green** dc12, **with dark green** dc3, 2dc in next, dc18, 2dc in next, sl st in first dc. (40)

Rnd 4: With dark green ch2, dc3, **with light green** dc13, **with dark green** dc3, 2dc in next, dc19, 2dc in next, sl st in first dc. (42)

Rnd 5: With dark green ch2, dc3, **with light green** dc14, **with dark green** dc3, 2dc in next, dc20, 2dc in next, sl st in first dc. (44)

Rnd 6: With dark green ch2, dc3, **with light green** dc15, **with dark green** dc3, 2dc in next, dc21, 2dc in next, sl st in first dc. (46)

Rnd 7: With dark green ch2, dc3, **with light green** dc16, **with dark green** dc3, 2dc in next, dc22, 2dc in next, sl st in first dc. (48)

Rnd 8: With dark green ch2, dc3, **with light green** dc17, **with dark green** dc3, 2dc in next, dc23, 2dc in next, sl st in first dc. (50)

Rnd 9: With dark green ch2, dc3, **with light green** dc18, **with dark green** dc3, 2dc in next, dc24, 2dc in next, sl st in first dc. (52)

Rnd 10: With dark green ch2, dc3, **with light green** dc19, **with dark green** dc3, 2dc in next, dc25, 2dc in next, sl st in first dc. (54)

Rnd 11: With dark green ch2, dc3, **with light green** dc20, **with dark green** dc3, 2dc in next, dc26, 2dc in next, sl st in first dc. (56)

Rnd 12: With dark green ch2, dc3, **with light green** dc21, **with dark green** dc3, 2dc in next, dc27, 2dc in next, sl st in first dc. (58)

Rnd 13: With dark green ch2, dc3, **with light green** dc22, **with dark green** dc3, 2dc in next, dc28, 2dc in next, sl st in first dc. (60)

Rnd 14: With dark green ch2, dc3, **with light green** dc23, **with dark green** dc3, 2dc in next, dc29, 2dc in next, sl st in first dc. (62)

Rnd 15: With dark green ch2, dc3, **with light green** dc24, **with dark green** dc3, 2dc in next, dc30, 2dc in next, sl st in first dc. (64)

Rnd 16: With dark green ch2, dc3, **with light green** dc25, **with dark green** dc3, 2dc in next, dc31, 2dc in next, sl st in first dc. (66)

Rnd 17: With dark green ch2, dc3, **with light green** dc26, **with dark green** dc3, 2dc in next, dc32, 2dc in next, sl st in first dc. (68)

Rnd 18: With dark green ch2, dc3, **with light green** dc27, **with dark green** dc3, 2dc in next, dc33, 2dc in next, sl st in first dc. (70)

Rnd 19: With dark green ch2, dc3, **with light green** dc28, **with dark green** dc3, 2dc in next, dc34, 2dc in next, sl st in first dc. (72)

Cut a long thread to close the body at the end; fold the body along the increase line.

ARMS (MAKE 2)

Rnd 1: With dark green (leave a long thread here to sew the arm in at the end) ch13, sl st in the first ch to form a ring, ch2 (does not count as first st), dc1 in each ch around, sl st in first dc. (13)

Rnd 2: Ch2, 2dc in first dc, dc1 in each stitch around, sl st in first dc. (14)

Rnd 3: Ch2, dc1 in each stitch all round, sl st in first dc. (14)

Rnd 4: Ch2, 2dc in first dc, dc1 in each stitch round, sl st in first dc. (15)

Rnd 5: Ch2, dc1 in each stitch around, sl st in first dc. (15)

Rnd 6: Ch2, 2dc in first dc, dc1 in each stitch around, sl st in first dc. (16)

Rnd 7: Ch2, dc1 in each stitch around, sl st in first dc. (16)

Rnd 8: Ch2, 2dc in first dc, dc1 in each stitch around, sl st in first dc. (17)

Rnd 9: Ch2, dc1 in each stitch around, sl st in first dc. (17)

Rnd 10: Ch2, 2dc in first dc, dc1 in each stitch around, sl st in first dc. (18)

Rnd 11: From now on, crochet in the round without fastening the rounds, sc1 each stitch around. (18)

Rnd 12: *Sc2, 2sc in next*, repeat from * to * around. (24)

Rnd 13–Rnd 19: Sc1 in each stitch around. (24)

Rnd 20: *Sc1, (in the following stitch: hdc1, dc1, tr1, dc1, hdc1), sc1, sl st*, repeat from * to * around. You will then have three fingers (6 repeats).
Cut a long thread and close the seam of the fingers.

LEGS (MAKE 2)

Rnd 1: With dark green ch14, sl st in the first ch to form a ring, ch2 (does not count as the first stitch), dc1 in each ch around, sl st in first dc. (14)

Rnd 2: Ch2, 2dc in first dc, dc1 in each stitch around, sl st in first dc. (15)

Rnd 3: Ch2, dc1 in each stitch around, sl st in first dc. (15)

Rnd 4: Ch2, 2dc in first dc, dc1 in each stitch around, sl st in first dc. (16)

Rnd 5: Ch2, dc1 in each stitch around, sl st in first dc. (16)

Rnd 6: Ch2, 2dc in first dc, dc1 in each stitch around, sl st in first dc. (17)

Rnd 7: Ch2, dc1 in each stitch around, sl st in first dc. (17)

Rnd 8: Ch2, 2dc in first dc, dc1 in every stitch around, sl st in first dc. (18)

Rnd 9: From now on, crochet in the round without fastening the rounds, sc1 in each stitch around. (18)

Rnd 10: *Sc2, 2sc in next*, repeat from * to * around. (24)

Rnd 11–Rnd 15: Sc1 in each stitch around. (24)

Rnd 16: *Sc1, (in the following stitch: hdc1, dc1, tr1, dc1, hdc1), sc1, sl st*, repeat from * to * around. You will then have three toes (6 repeats).
Cut a long thread and close the toe seam.

PUTTING IT ALL TOGETHER

- Place each leg between the two layers at the bottom of the body. Use the remaining yarn to sew along the bottom with the two feet in between to close the seam while at the same time attaching the parts.
- Sew an arm on either side of the body between Rnd 1 and Rnd 3.
- Sew Rnd 14 of the head on Rnd 1 of the body.

BABY FROG

This baby frog will hop right into your hands for a squeeze.

DIMENSIONS

6.3 in. (16 cm) long and 3.9 in. (10 cm) wide

MATERIALS

DK #3 lightweight yarn (sample shown in Scheepjes Stone Washed):
• light green (New Jade): 55 yd. (50 m)
• dark green (Canada Jade): 109 yd. (100 m)
Crochet hook: US size D-3 (3 mm)
Gold and black safety eyes, 12 mm
Fiberfill stuffing
Needle and scissors

DIFFICULTY LEVEL

EYES (MAKE 2)

Rnd 1: With dark green, start with a magic ring, 6sc in the ring. (6)
Rnd 2: 2sc in each stitch around. (12)
Rnd 3: *Sc2, 2sc in next*, repeat from * to * around. (16)
Rnd 4–Rnd 5: Sc1 in each stitch around. (16)
For the first eye, tie the thread off; for the second eye, let the thread hang and continue with the head.

HEAD

The eyes are connected and form the top of the head.
Rnd 1: With dark green, continue with the second eye, sc7, take the first eye and crochet the next stitch of the second eye and the first eye together, sc14,

crochet the next stitch of the first and second eye together, sc7. (30)

Rnd 2: *Sc4, 2sc in next*, repeat from * to * around. (36)

Rnd 3–Rnd 5: Sc1 in each stitch around. (36)

Rnd 6: With dark green sc4, **with light green** sc10, **with dark green** sc22. (36)

Rnd 7: With dark green sc5, **with light green** sc9, **with dark green** sc22. (36)

Rnd 8: With dark green sc6, **with light green** sc8, **with dark green** sc22. (36)

Rnd 9: With dark green sc7, **with light green** sc7, **with dark green** sc22. (36)

Rnd 10: With dark green sc4, sc2tog, sc2, **with light green** sc2, sc2tog, sc2, **with dark green** sc2, sc2tog, *sc4, sc2tog*, repeat from * to * to end. (30)

Rnd 11: With dark green sc3, sc2tog, sc3, **with light green** sc2tog, sc2, **with dark green** sc1, sc2tog, *sc3, sc2tog*, repeat from * to * to end. (24)

Rnd 12: With dark green *sc2, sc2tog*, repeat from * to * 1 more time, **with light green** sc2, **with dark green** sc2tog, *sc2, sc2tog*, repeat from * to * to end. (18)

At this point, attach the eyes between Rnd 5 of the eye and Rnd 1 of the head and fill the head.

Rnd 13: With dark green *sc1, sc2tog*, repeat from * to * 1 more time, sc1, **with light green** sc1, **with dark green** (sc2tog) 2 times, *sc1, sc2tog*, repeat from * to * to end. (12)

Cut the thread, close the seam **with the dark green** thread, and weave in the **light green** thread neatly.

BODY

Rnd 1: With dark green ch13, dc1 in third ch from hook, dc9, 3dc in last ch, continue along other side of chains, dc10, 3dc in last ch, sl st in first dc. (26)

Rnd 2: Ch2 (does not count as first stitch for the entire pattern), *dc12, 2dc in the following*, repeat from * to * 1 more time, sl st in first st. (28)

Rnd 3: Ch2, dc3; **with light green** dc7, **with dark green** dc3, 2dc in next, dc13, 2dc in next, sl st in first dc. (30)

Rnd 4: With dark green ch2, dc3, **with light green** dc8, **with dark green** dc3, 2dc in the next, dc14, 2dc in the next, sl st in first dc. (32)

Rnd 5: With dark green ch2, dc3, **with light green** dc9, **with dark green** dc2, 2dc in next, dc15, 2dc in next, sl st in first dc. (34)

Rnd 6: With dark green ch2, dc3, **with light green** dc10, **with dark green** dc3, 2dc in next, dc16, 2dc in next, sl st in first dc. (36)

Rnd 7: With dark green ch2, dc3, **with light green** dc11, **with dark green** dc3, 2dc in next, dc17, 2dc in next, sl st in first dc. (38)

Rnd 8: With dark green ch2, dc3, **with light green** dc12, **with dark green** dc3, 2dc in next, dc18, 2dc in next, sl st in first dc. (40)

Rnd 9: With dark green ch2, dc3, **with light green** dc13, **with dark green** dc3, 2dc in next, dc19, 2dc in next, sl st in first dc. (42)

Rnd 10: With dark green ch2, dc3, **with light green** dc14, **with dark green** dc3, 2dc in next, dc20, 2dc in next, sl st in first dc. (44)

Rnd 11: With dark green ch2, dc3, **with light green** dc15, **with dark green** dc3, 2dc in next, dc21, 2dc in next, sl st in first dc. (46)

Cut the **light green** thread and weave in the end.

Rnd 12: Ch2, *dc22, ch14, dc1 in third ch from hook, dc1 in each of the 11 remaining chs, 2dc in the next stitch on Rnd 11*, repeat from * to * 1 more time, sl st in first st. Cut a long thread to close the body later.

ARMS (MAKE 2)

Rnd 1: With dark green (leave a long thread here to sew the arm at the end) ch9, sl st in the first ch to form a ring, ch2 (does not count as first dc), dc1 in each ch around, sl st in first dc. (9)

Rnd 2: Ch2, 2dc in first dc, dc1 in each stitch around, sl st in first dc. (10)

Rnd 3: Ch2, dc1 in each stitch around, sl st in first dc. (10)

Rnd 4: Ch2, 2dc in first dc, dc1 in each stitch around, sl st in first dc. (11)

Rnd 5: Ch2, dc1 in each stitch round, sl st in first dc. (11)

Rnd 6: Ch2, 2dc in first dc, dc1 in each stitch around, sl st in first dc. (12)

Rnd 7: From now on hook in continuous rounds without closing the rounds, sc1 in each stitch around. (12)

Rnd 8: *Sc1, 2sc in next*, repeat from * to * around. (18)

Rnd 9–Rnd 10: Sc1 in each stitch around. (18)

Rnd 11: *Sc1, (in next stitch: hdc1, dc1, tr1, dc1, hdc1), sl st *, repeat from * to * all around; you will have three fingers (6 repeats). Cut a long thread and sew the seam of the fingers closed.

PUTTING IT ALL TOGETHER

- Fold the body along the increase lines and use the remaining thread from the body to close the bottom.
- Make a knot in the corners to make the feet.
- Sew an arm on each side of the body between Rnd 1 and Rnd 2.

- Finally, sew Rnd 8 of the head (eyes not counted) to Rnd 1 of the body.

HIPPO

This little one will relax with you anytime.

DIMENSIONS

12.2 in. (31 cm) long and 5.9 in. (15 cm) wide

MATERIALS

DK #3 lightweight yarn (sample shown in Scheepjes Stone Washed):
• purple (Deep Amethyst): 218.7 yd. (200 m)
Crochet hook: US size D-3 (3 mm)
Black and blue safety eyes, 15 mm
Black safety eyes, 10 mm (for nostrils)
Fiberfill stuffing
Yarn needle and scissors

DIFFICULTY LEVEL

HEAD

Rnd 1: Start with a magic ring, 6sc in the loop. (6)
Rnd 2: 2sc in each stitch around. (12)
Rnd 3: *Sc1, 2sc in next*, repeat from * to * around. (18)
Rnd 4: *Sc2, 2sc in next*, repeat from * to * around. (24)
Rnd 5: *Sc3, 2sc in next*, repeat from * to * around. (30)
Rnd 6: *Sc4, 2sc in next*, repeat from * to * around. (36)
Rnd 7: *Sc5, 2sc in next*, repeat from * to * around. (42)
Rnd 8: *Sc6, 2sc in next*, repeat from * to * around. (48)
Rnd 9–Rnd 20: Sc1 in each stitch around. (48)
Rnd 21: *2sc in each of the next 3 stitches, sc21*, repeat from * to * one more time. (54)

Rnd 22: *2sc in each of the next 6 stitches, sc21*, repeat from * to * one more time. (66)

Attach the black and blue safety eyes between Rnd 19 and Rnd 20, 11 stitches apart.

Rnd 23–Rnd 27: Sc1 in each stitch around. (66)

Rnd 28: *Sc9, sc2tog*, repeat from * to * around. (60)

Rnd 29: Sc1 in each stitch around. (60)

Rnd 30: *Sc8, sc2tog*, repeat from * to * around. (54)

Rnd 31: Sc1 in each stitch around. (54)

Rnd 32: *Sc7, sc2tog*, repeat from * to * around. (48)

Rnd 33: *Sc6, sc2tog*, repeat from * to * around. (42)

Rnd 34: *Sc5, sc2tog*, repeat from * to * around. (36)

Rnd 35: *Sc4, sc2tog*, repeat from * to * around. (30)

Rnd 36: *Sc3, sc2tog*, repeat from * to * around. (24)

Rnd 37: *Sc2, sc2tog*, repeat from * to * around. (18)

Attach the nostrils (black safety eyes) between Rnd 30 and Rnd 31, 11 stitches apart; stuff the head.

Rnd 38: *Sc1, sc2tog*, repeat from * to * around. (12)

Cut yarn, close the seam, and weave in ends.

EARS (MAKE 2)

Row 1: Start with a magic ring, 6sc in the loop. (6) You won't close this row, but continue working flat.

Row 2: Turn, ch1 (doesn't count as first stitch for entire ear), sc1, 2dc in each of the next 4 stitches, sc1 in last. (10)

Row 3: Turn, ch1, 2sc in first sc, 1dc in each of the next 8 stitches, 2sc in last. (12)

Cut a long thread, sew ears closed on the bottom (these are the first and last sc of the rows), and attach to each side of the head against Rnd 7.

BODY

Rnd 1: Ch18, 1dc in third ch from hook, dc14, 3dc in last, continue along other side of chains, dc15, 3dc in last, sl st in first dc. (36)

Rnd 2: Ch2 (doesn't count as first stitch now and throughout), *dc17, 2dc in next*, repeat from * to * one more time, sl st in first dc. (38)

Rnd 3: Ch2, *dc18, 2dc in next*, repeat from * to * one more time, sl st in first dc. (40)

Rnd 4: Ch2, *dc19, 2dc in next*, repeat from * to * one more time, sl st in first dc. (42)

Rnd 5: Ch2, *dc20, 2dc in next*, repeat from * to * one more time, sl st in first dc. (44)

Rnd 6: Ch2, *dc21, 2dc in next*, repeat from * to * one more time, sl st in first dc. (46)

Rnd 7: Ch2, *dc22, 2dc in next*, repeat from * to * one more time, sl st in first dc. (48)

Rnd 8: Ch2, *dc23, 2dc in next*, repeat from * to * one more time, sl st in first dc. (50)

Rnd 9: Ch2, *dc24, 2dc in next*, repeat from * to * one more time, sl st in first dc. (52)

Rnd 10: Ch2, *dc25, 2dc in next*, repeat from * to * one more time, sl st in first dc. (54)

Rnd 11: Ch2, *dc26, 2dc in next*, repeat from * to * one more time, sl st in first dc. (56)

Rnd 12: Ch2, *dc27, 2dc in next*, repeat from * to * one more time, sl st in first dc. (58)

Rnd 13: Ch2, *dc28, 2dc in next*, repeat from * to * one more time, sl st in first dc. (60)

Rnd 14: Ch2, *dc29, 2dc in next*, repeat from * to * one more time, sl st in first dc. (62)

Rnd 15: Ch2, *dc30, 2dc in next*, repeat from * to * one more time, sl st in first dc. (64)

Rnd 16: Ch2, *dc31, 2dc in next*, repeat from * to * one more time, sl st in first dc. (66)

Rnd 17: Ch2, *dc32, 2dc in next*, repeat from * to * one more time, sl st in first dc. (68)

Rnd 18: Ch2, *dc33, 2dc in next*, repeat from * to * one more time, sl st in first dc. (70)

Rnd 19: Ch2, *dc34, 2dc in next*, repeat from * to * one more time, sl st in first dc. (72)

Cut a long tail to close the body in the end. Fold the body in line with the increases to make the belly straight.

ARMS (MAKE 2)

Rnd 1: Start with a magic ring, 6sc in the loop. (6)

Rnd 2: 2sc in each stitch around. (12)

Rnd 3: *Sc1, 2sc in next*, repeat from * to * around. (18)

Rnd 4: *Sc2, 2sc in next*, repeat from * to * around. (24)

Rnd 5–Rnd 9: Sc1 in each stitch around. (24)

Rnd 10: *Sc2, sc2tog*, repeat from * to * around. (18)

Rnd 11–Rnd 12: Sc1 in each stitch around. (18)

Rnd 13: Sl st, ch2 (doesn't count as first stitch now and throughout), dc1 in each stitch around, sl st in first dc. (18)

Rnd 14: Ch2, dc2tog, dc1 in each stitch around, sl st in first dc. (17)

At this point, stuff the hand, take a piece of purple yarn, and sew across the arm between Rnd 12 and Rnd 13.

Rnd 15: Ch2, dc1 in each stitch around, sl st in first dc. (17)

Rnd 16: Ch2, dc2tog, dc1 in each stitch around, sl st in first dc. (16)

Rnd 17: Ch2, dc1 in each stitch around, sl st in first dc. (16)

Rnd 18: Ch2, dc2tog, dc1 in each stitch around, sl st in first dc. (15)

Rnd 19: Ch2, dc1 in each stitch around, sl st in first dc. (15)

Rnd 20: Ch2, dc2tog, dc1 in each stitch around, sl st in first dc. (14)

Rnd 21: Ch2, dc1 in each stitch around, sl st in first dc. (14)

Rnd 22: Ch2, dc2tog, dc1 in each stitch around, sl st in first dc. (13)
Cut a long tail to attach arms later.

FEET (MAKE 2)

Rnd 1: Start with a magic ring, ch2 (doesn't count as first stitch now and throughout), 12dc in the loop, sl st in first dc. (12)
Rnd 2: Ch2, *dc1, 2dc in next*, repeat around from * to *, sl st in first dc. (18)
Rnd 3–Rnd 7: Ch2, dc1 in each stitch around, sl st in first dc. (18) Cut the yarn and weave in ends.

PUTTING IT ALL TOGETHER

- Place both legs between the bottom two layers of the body and use the remaining yarn from the body to sew across the seam, with legs in between, to close and at the same time attach the parts.
- Sew an arm to each side of the body between Rnd 1 and Rnd 3.
- Sew Rnd 25 of the head to Rnd 1 of the body.

HIPPO CALF

This little hippo is ready to play by the water instead of in it.

DIMENSIONS

6.7 in. (17 cm) long and 3.9 in. (10 cm) wide

MATERIALS

DK #3 lightweight yarn (sample shown in Scheepjes Stone Washed):
• purple (Lilac Quartz): 142.2 yd. (130 m)
Crochet hook: US size D-3 (3 mm)
Blue and black safety eyes, 15 mm
Fiberfill stuffing
Yarn needle and scissors

DIFFICULTY LEVEL

HEAD

Rnd 1: Start with a magic ring, 6sc in the ring. (6)
Rnd 2: 2sc in each stitch around. (12)
Rnd 3: *Sc1, 2sc in next*, repeat from * to * around. (18)
Rnd 4: *Sc2, 2sc in next*, repeat from * to * around. (24)
Rnd 5: *Sc3, 2sc in next*, repeat from * to * around. (30)
Rnd 6: *Sc4, 2sc in next*, repeat from * to * around. (36)
Rnd 7–Rnd 14: Sc1 in each stitch around. (36)
Rnd 15: *2sc in each of the following 2 stitches, sc16*, repeat from * to * 1 more time. (40)
Rnd 16: *2sc in each of the following 4 stitches, sc16*, repeat from * to * 1 more time. (48)

Attach the blue and black eyes between Rnd 14 and Rnd 15 with 7 stitches in between.

Rnd 17–Rnd 18: Sc1 in each stitch around. (48)

Rnd 19: *Sc6, sc2tog*, repeat from * to * around. (42)

Rnd 20: Sc1 in each stitch around. (42)

Rnd 21: *Sc5, sc2tog*, repeat from * to * around. (36)

Rnd 22: Sc1 in each stitch around. (36)

Rnd 23: *Sc4, sc2tog*, repeat from * to * around. (30)

Rnd 24: *Sc3, sc2tog*, repeat from * to * around. (24)

Rnd 25: *Sc2, sc2tog*, repeat from * to * around. (18) Now attach the black safety eyes for the nostrils between Rnd 21 and Rnd 22 with 7 stitches in between and fill the head.

Rnd 26: *Sc1, sc2tog*, repeat from * to * around. (12) Cut the thread, close the seam, and weave in the yarn.

EARS (MAKE 2)

Start with a magic ring, 6sc in the ring; do not close this rnd, but turn and work back. (6)

Ch1 (does not count as first stitch), sc1, 2dc in each of the 4 following stitches, sc1 in the last. (10)

Cut a long thread and sew up the ears at the bottom (the first and the last sc of the rows). Let the yarn hang to secure the ears later.

BODY

Rnd 1: Ch13, dc1 in third ch from hook, dc9, 3dc in last, continue along other side of chains, dc10, 3dc in last, sl st in first dc. (26)

Rnd 2: Ch2 (does not count as the first dc from now on), *dc12, 2dc in the next*, repeat from * to * 1 more time, sl st in first dc. (28)

Rnd 3: Ch2, *dc13, 2dc in next*, repeat from * to * 1 more time, sl st in first dc. (30)

Rnd 4: Ch2, *dc14, 2dc in next*, repeat from * to * 1 more time, sl st in first dc. (32)

Rnd 5: Ch2, *dc15, 2dc in next*, repeat from * to * 1 more time, sl st in first dc. (34)

Rnd 6: Ch2, *dc16, 2dc in next*, repeat from * to * 1 more time, sl st in first dc. (36)

Rnd 7: Ch2, *dc17, 2dc in next*, repeat from * to * 1 more time, sl st in first dc. (38)

Rnd 8: Ch2, *dc18, 2dc in next*, repeat from * to * 1 more time, sl st in first dc. (40)

Rnd 9: Ch2, *dc19, 2dc in next*, repeat from * to * 1 more time, sl st in first dc. (42)

Rnd 10: Ch2, *dc20, 2dc in next*, repeat from * to * 1 more time, sl st in first dc. (44)

Rnd 11: Ch2, *dc21, 2dc in next*, repeat from * to * 1 more time, sl st in first dc. (46)

Rnd 12: Ch2, *dc22, ch14, dc1 in 3rd ch from hook, dc1 in each of the 11 remaining chs, 2dc in the next stitch on Rnd 11*, repeat from * to * 1 more time, sl st in first st.

Cut a long thread to close the body later.

ARMS (MAKE 2)

Rnd 1: Start with a magic ring, 6sc in the ring. (6)

Rnd 2: 2sc in each stitch around. (12)

Rnd 3: *Sc1, 2sc in next*, repeat from * to * around. (18)

Rnd 4–Rnd 5: Sc1 in each stitch around. (18)

Rnd 6: *Sc1, sc2tog*, repeat from * to * around. (12)

Rnd 7: Sc1 in each stitch around. (12)

Rnd 8: Sl st, ch2 (does not count as first dc from now on), dc1 in every stitch around, sl st in first dc. (12)

Rnd 9: Ch2, dc2tog, dc1 in each stitch around, sl st in first dc. (11)

Now stuff the hand, and then take a piece of yarn and sew along the hand between Rnd 7 and Rnd 8.

Rnd 10: Ch2, dc1 in each stitch around, sl st in first dc. (11)

Rnd 11: Ch2, dc2tog, dc1 in each stitch around, sl st in first dc. (10)

Rnd 12: Ch2, dc1 in each stitch around, sl st in first dc. (10)

Rnd 13: Ch2, dc2tog, dc1 in each stitch around, sl st in first dc. (9)

Cut and leave a long thread to secure the arms later.

PUTTING IT ALL TOGETHER

- Sew the ears to the sides of the head in Rnd 5.
- Fold the body neatly on the increase lines and close the bottom.
- Make a knot in the corners to make the feet.
- Sew an arm on each side of the body between Rnd 1 and Rnd 2.
- Sew Rnd 23 of the head to Rnd 1 of the body.

KANGAROO

This mama kangaroo has a pouch for her joey or a secret treasure.

DIMENSIONS

11.4 in. (29 cm) long and 6.3 in. (16 cm) wide

MATERIALS

DK #3 lightweight yarn (sample shown in Scheepjes Stone Washed):
• beige (Boulder Opal): 218.7 yd. (200 m)
• white (Moon Stone): 76.6 yd. (70 m)
Crochet hook: US size D-3 (3 mm)
Black safety eyes, 15 mm
Black safety nose, 15 mm
Fiberfill stuffing
Yarn needle and scissors

DIFFICULTY LEVEL

HEAD

Rnd 1: With beige, start with a magic ring, 6sc in the loop. (6)
Rnd 2: 2sc in each stitch around. (12)
Rnd 3: *Sc1, 2sc in next*, repeat from * to * around. (18)
Rnd 4: *Sc2, 2sc in next*, repeat from * to * around. (24)
Rnd 5: *Sc3, 2sc in next*, repeat from * to * around. (30)
Rnd 6: *Sc4, 2sc in next*, repeat from * to * around. (36)
Rnd 7: *Sc5, 2sc in next*, repeat from * to * around. (42)
Rnd 8–Rnd 15: Sc1 in each stitch around. (42)
Rnd 16: 3sc in next stitch, sc3, 3sc in next stitch, sc37. (46)

Rnd 17: Sc1, 3sc in next stitch, sc5, 3sc in next stitch, sc38. (50)
Rnd 18: Sc2, 3sc in next stitch, sc7, 3sc in next stitch, sc39. (54)
Rnd 19–Rnd 23: Sc1 in each stitch around. (54)

Attach the safety eyes between Rnd 15 and Rnd 16 on both sides of the snout with 8 stitches between them. Attach the safety nose between Rnd 20 and Rnd 21 in the center of the snout.

Rnd 24: *Sc7, sc2tog*, repeat from * to * around. (48)
Rnd 25: *Sc6, sc2tog*, repeat from * to * around. (42)
Rnd 26: *Sc5, sc2tog*, repeat from * to * around. (36)
Rnd 27: *Sc4, sc2tog*, repeat from * to * around. (30)
Rnd 28: *Sc3, sc2tog*, repeat from * to * around. (24)
Rnd 29: *Sc2, sc2tog*, repeat from * to * around. (18) Stuff the head.
Rnd 30: *Sc1, sc2tog*, repeat from * to * around. (12)

Cut a long thread, close the seam, and weave in ends.

EARS (MAKE 2)

Rnd 1: With beige, start with a magic ring, ch2 (doesn't count as first dc now and throughout), 12dc in the loop, sl st in first dc. (12)
Rnd 2: Ch2, dc1, 5dc in next, dc4, 5dc in next, dc4, 5dc in next, sl st in first dc. (24)
Rnd 3: Ch2, dc3, 5dc in next, dc8, 5dc in next, dc8, 5dc in next, dc2, sl st in first dc. (36)

Cut a long thread, fold the bottom (the side with the least dc, so the side where your yarn is attached), and sew the bottom closed; let the yarn end hang to attach ears later.

BODY

Rnd 1: With beige ch18, 1dc in third ch from hook, dc14, 3dc in last, continue along other side of chains, dc15, 3dc in last, sl st in first dc. (36)
Rnd 2: Ch2 (doesn't count as first dc now and throughout), dc3, **with white** dc11, **with beige** dc3, 2dc in next, dc17, 2dc in next, sl st in first dc. (38)
Rnd 3: With beige ch2, dc3, **with white** dc12, **with beige** dc3, 2dc in next, dc18, 2dc in next, sl st in first dc. (40)
Rnd 4: With beige ch2, dc3, **with white** dc13, **with beige** dc3, 2dc in next, dc19, 2dc in next, sl st in first dc. (42)
Rnd 5: With beige ch2, dc3, **with white** dc14, **with beige** dc3, 2dc in next, dc20, 2dc in next, sl st in first dc. (44)
Rnd 6: With beige ch2, dc3, **with white** dc15, **with beige** dc3, 2dc in next, dc21, 2dc in next, sl st in first dc. (46)

Rnd 7: With beige ch2, dc3, **with white** dc16, **with beige** dc3, 2dc in next, dc22, 2dc in next, sl st in first dc. (48)

Rnd 8: With beige ch2, dc3, **with white** dc17, **with beige** dc3, 2dc in next, dc23, 2dc in next, sl st in first dc. (50)

Rnd 9: With beige ch2, dc3, **with white** dc18, **with beige** dc3, 2dc in next, dc24, 2dc in next, sl st in first dc. (52)

Rnd 10: With beige ch2, dc3, **with white** dc19, **with beige** dc3, 2dc in next, dc25, 2dc in next, sl st in first dc. (54)

Rnd 11: With beige ch2, dc3, **with white** dc20, **with beige** dc3, 2dc in next, dc26, 2dc in next, sl st in first dc. (56)

Rnd 12: With beige ch2, dc3, **with white** dc21, **with beige** dc3, 2dc in next, dc27, 2dc in next, sl st in first dc. (58)

Rnd 13: With beige ch2, dc3, **with white** dc22, **with beige** dc3, 2dc in next, dc28, 2dc in next, sl st in first dc. (60)

From now on you'll continue with beige; you can cut the white yarn.

Rnd 14: Ch2, *dc29, 2dc in next*, repeat from * to * one more time, sl st in first dc. (62)

Rnd 15: Ch2, *dc30, 2dc in next*, repeat from * to * one more time, sl st in first dc. (64)

Rnd 16: Ch2, *dc31, 2dc in next*, repeat from * to * one more time, sl st in first dc. (66)

Rnd 17: Ch2, *dc32, 2dc in next*, repeat from * to * one more time, sl st in first dc. (68)

Rnd 18: Ch2, *dc33, 2dc in next*, repeat from * to * one more time, sl st in first dc. (70)

Rnd 19: Ch2, *dc34, 2dc in next*, repeat from * to * one more time, sl st in first dc. (72)

Rnd 20: Ch2, *dc35, 2dc in next*, repeat from * to * one more time, sl st in first dc. (74)

Rnd 21: Ch2, *dc36, 2dc in next*, repeat from * to * one more time, sl st in first dc. (76)

Cut a long thread to close the body in the end; fold the body in line with the increases on the side.

ARMS (MAKE 2)

Rnd 1: With beige, start with a magic ring, 6sc in the loop. (6)

Rnd 2: 2sc in each stitch around. (12)

Rnd 3: *Sc1, 2sc in next*, repeat from * to * around. (18)

Rnd 4: *Sc2, 2sc in next*, repeat from * to * around. (24)

Rnd 5–Rnd 9: Sc1 in each stitch around. (24)

Rnd 10: *Sc2, sc2tog*, repeat from * to * around. (18)

Rnd 11–Rnd 12: Sc1 in each stitch around. (18)

Cut a long thread; you'll use it after Rnd 14.

Rnd 13: Sl st 1, ch2 (doesn't count as first stitch now and throughout), dc1 in each stitch around, sl st in first dc. (18)

Rnd 14: Ch2, dc2tog, dc1 in each stitch around, sl st in first dc. (17)

At this point, stuff the hand. Take the remaining yarn and sew across the arm between Rnd 12 and Rnd 13.

Rnd 15: Ch2, dc1 in each stitch around, sl st in first dc. (17)

Rnd 16: Ch2, dc2tog, dc1 in each stitch around, sl st in first dc. (16)

Rnd 17: Ch2, dc1 in each stitch around, sl st in first dc. (16)

Rnd 18: Ch2, dc2tog, dc1 in each stitch around, sl st in first dc. (15)

Rnd 19: Ch2, dc1 in each stitch around, sl st in first dc. (15)

Rnd 20: Ch2, dc2tog, dc1 in each stitch around, sl st in first dc. (14)

Rnd 21: Ch2, dc1 in each stitch around, sl st in first dc. (14)

Rnd 22: Ch2, dc2tog, dc1 in each stitch around, sl st in first dc. (13)

Cut a long tail to attach the arms to the body later.

LEGS (MAKE 2)

Rnd 1: With beige, start with a magic ring, ch2 (doesn't count as first stitch now and throughout), dc12 in the loop, sl st in first dc. (12)

Rnd 2: Ch2, *dc1, 2dc in next*, repeat from * to * around, sl st in first dc. (18)

Rnd 3–Rnd 4: Ch2, dc1 in each stitch around, sl st in first dc. (18)

Cut the yarn and weave in the ends.

POUCH

Note: This isn't crocheted in the round.

Row 1: With beige, start with a magic ring, ch2 (doesn't count as first stitch now and throughout), dc8. (8)

Row 2: Ch2, turn, dc1, 2dc in each of the next 6dc, dc1. (14)

Row 3: Ch2, turn, dc1, *dc1, 2dc in next*, repeat from * to * 5 more times, dc1. (20)

Row 4: Ch2, turn, dc1, *dc2, 2dc in next*, repeat from * to * 5 more times, dc1. (26)

Row 5: Ch2, turn, dc1, *dc3, 2dc in next*, repeat from * to * 5 more times, dc1. (32)

Row 6: Ch2, turn, dc1, *dc4, 2dc in next*, repeat from * to * 5 more times, dc1. (38)

Row 7: Instead of turning, continue along the top side of the pouch; this is actually on the side of the rows you just made, ch3, 2dc on the side of each row (you'll crochet this around the side of the double crochets and the chain twos on the side). End with 1dc in the first dc of row 6.

Cut a long thread to attach the pouch to the body in the end.

TAIL

Rnd 1: With beige, start with a magic ring, ch2 (doesn't count as first stitch now and throughout), 12dc in the loop, sl st in first dc. (12)

Rnd 2: Ch2, *dc3, 5dc in next*, repeat from * to * around, sl st in first dc. (24)

Rnd 3: Ch2, dc5, 5dc in next, *dc7, 5dc in next*, repeat from * to * 1 more time, dc2, sl st in first dc. (36)

Rnd 4: Ch2, dc7, 5dc in next, *dc11, 5dc in next*, repeat from * to * 1 more time, dc4, sl st in first dc. (48)

Rnd 5: Ch2, dc9, 5dc in next, *dc15, 5dc in next*, repeat from * to * 1 more time, dc6, sl st in first dc. (60)

Rnd 6: Ch2, dc11, 5dc in next, *dc19, 5dc in next*, repeat from * to * 1 more time, dc8, sl st in first dc. (72)

Cut a long thread to close the tail and attach it to the body in the end.

PUTTING IT ALL TOGETHER

- Sew the pouch to the belly from Rnd 13 to Rnd 21.
- Place both legs in the bottom two layers of the body. With the remaining yarn from the body, sew across the seam with the parts in between. This way you close the bottom and assemble the pieces at the same time.
- Sew an arm to each side of the body between Rnd 1 and Rnd 3.
- Sew the ears to each side of the head in Rnd 7; they are 6 stitches apart on the back.
- Fold the tail in half, sew closed, and sew the tail to the bottom 6 rounds of the body.
- Finally, sew Rnd 24 of the head to Rnd 1 of the body.

JOEY

DIMENSIONS

6.3 in. (16 cm) long by 3.9 in. (10 cm) wide

MATERIALS

DK #3 lightweight yarn (sample shown in Scheepjes Stone Washed):
• beige (Boulder Opal): 142.2 yd. (130 m)
Crochet hook: US size D-3 (3 mm)
Black safety eyes, 12 mm
Black safety nose, 15 mm
Fiberfill stuffing
Yarn needle and scissors

DIFFICULTY LEVEL

HEAD

Rnd 1: Start with a magic ring, 6sc in the loop. (6)
Rnd 2: 2sc in each stitch around. (12)
Rnd 3: *Sc1, 2sc in next*, repeat from * to * around. (18)
Rnd 4: *Sc2, 2sc in next*, repeat from * to * around. (24)
Rnd 5: *Sc3, 2sc in next*, repeat from * to * around. (30)
Rnd 6–Rnd 10: Sc1 in each stitch around. (30)
Rnd 11: 3sc in next stitch, sc1, 3sc in next stitch, sc27. (34)
Rnd 12: Sc1, 3sc in next stitch, sc3, 3sc in next stitch, sc28. (38)
Rnd 13: Sc2, 3sc in next stitch, sc5, 3sc in next stitch, sc29. (42)
Rnd 14–Rnd 17: Sc1 in each stitch around. (42)
Attach the safety eyes between Rnd 10 and Rnd 11 on each side of the snout with 6 stitches between them. Attach the safety nose between Rnd 14 and Rnd 15 in the center of the snout.

Rnd 18: *Sc5, sc2tog*, repeat from * to * around. (36)
Rnd 19: *Sc4, sc2tog*, repeat from * to * around. (30)
Rnd 20: *Sc3, sc2tog*, repeat from * to * around. (24)
Rnd 21: *Sc2, sc2tog*, repeat from * to * around. (18)
Cut a long thread, close the seam, and weave in the ends.

EARS (MAKE 2)

Rnd 1: Start with a magic ring, ch2 (doesn't count as first dc now and throughout), 12dc in the loop, sl st in first dc. (12)
Rnd 2: Ch2, dc1, 5dc in next, dc4, 5dc in next, dc4, 5dc in next, sl st in first dc. (24)
Cut a long thread, fold the bottom (the side where your yarn is attached), and sew the bottom closed; let the yarn end hang to attach the ears later.

BODY

Rnd 1: Ch13, dc1 in third ch from hook, dc9, 3dc in last, continue along other side of chains, dc10, 3dc in last, sl st in first dc. (26)
Rnd 2: Ch2 (doesn't count as first stitch now and throughout), *dc12, 2dc in next* repeat from * to * one more time, sl st in first dc. (28)
Rnd 3: Ch2, *dc13, 2dc in next*, repeat from * to * one more time, sl st in first dc. (30)
Rnd 4: Ch2, *dc14, 2dc in next*, repeat from * to * one more time, sl st in first dc. (32)
Rnd 5: Ch2, *dc15, 2dc in next*, repeat from * to * one more time, sl st in first dc. (34)
Rnd 6: Ch2, *dc16, 2dc in next*, repeat from * to * one more time, sl st in first dc. (36)
Rnd 7: Ch2, *dc17, 2dc in next*, repeat from * to * one more time, sl st in first dc. (38)
Rnd 8: Ch2, *dc18, 2dc in next*, repeat from * to * one more time, sl st in first dc. (40)
Rnd 9: Ch2, *dc19, 2dc in next*, repeat from * to * one more time, sl st in first dc. (42)
Rnd 10: Ch2, *dc20, 2dc in next*, repeat from * to * one more time, sl st in first dc. (44)
Rnd 11: Ch2, *dc21, 2dc in next*, repeat from * to * one more time, sl st in first dc. (46)
Rnd 12: Ch2, *dc22, ch14, dc1 in third ch from hook, dc1 in each of the remaining 11 chains, 2dc in next stitch of Rnd 11*, repeat from * to * one more time, sl st in first dc. Cut a long tail to close the body later.

ARMS (MAKE 2)

Rnd 1: Start with a magic ring, 6sc in the loop. (6)

Rnd 2: 2sc in each stitch around. (12)

Rnd 3: *Sc1, 2sc in next*, repeat from * to * around. (18)

Rnd 4–Rnd 5: Sc1 in each stitch around. (18)

Rnd 6: *Sc1, sc2tog*, repeat from * to * around. (12)

Rnd 7: Sc1 in each stitch around. (12) Cut a long thread; you'll use it after Rnd 9.

Rnd 8: Sl st 1, ch2 (doesn't count as first stitch now and throughout), dc1 in each stitch around, sl st in first dc. (12)

Rnd 9: Ch2, dc2tog, dc1 in each stitch around, sl st in first dc. (11)

At this point, stuff the hand. Take the remaining yarn and sew across the arm between Rnd 7 and Rnd 8.

Rnd 10: Ch2, dc1 in each stitch around, sl st in first dc. (11)

Rnd 11: Ch2, dc2tog, dc1 in each stitch around, sl st in first dc. (10)

Rnd 12: Ch2, dc1 in each stitch around, sl st in first dc. (10)

Rnd 13: Ch2, dc2tog, dc1 in each stitch around, sl st in first dc. (9)

Cut a long tail to attach the arms to the body later.

TAIL

Rnd 1: Start with a magic ring, ch2 (doesn't count as first stitch now and throughout), dc12 in the loop, sl st in first dc. (12)

Rnd 2: Ch2, *dc3, 5dc in next*, repeat from * to * around, sl st in first dc. (24)

Rnd 3: Ch2, dc5, 5dc in next, *dc7, 5dc in next*, repeat from * to * 1 more time, dc2, sl st in first dc. (36)

Cut a long thread to close the tail and to attach it to the body in the end.

PUTTING IT ALL TOGETHER

- Fold the body in line with the increases to make the belly straight; sew closed with the remaining yarn. Tie a knot in the corners to form the feet.
- Sew an arm to each side of the body between Rnd 1 and Rnd 3.
- Sew an ear to each side of the head in Rnd 4; on the back they are 6 stitches apart.
- Fold the tail in half, sew closed, and then sew the tail to the body from Rnd 9 to Rnd 11.

- Finally, sew Rnd 18 of the head to Rnd 1 of the body.

MONKEY

You will want to share a banana with this cute monkey.

DIMENSIONS

11 in. (28 cm) long and 5.9 in. (15 cm) wide

MATERIALS

DK #3 lightweight yarn (sample shown in Scheepjes Stone Washed):
• brown (Brown Agate): 218.7 yd. (200 m)
• pink (Pink Quartzite): 76.6 yd. (70 m)
Crochet hook: US size D-3 (3 mm)
Black and blue safety eyes, 15 mm
Fiberfill stuffing
Yarn needle and scissors

DIFFICULTY LEVEL

HEAD

Rnd 1: With brown, start with a magic ring, 6sc in the loop. (6)
Rnd 2: 2sc in each stitch around. (12)
Rnd 3: *Sc1, 2sc in next*, repeat from * to * around. (18)
Rnd 4: *Sc2, 2sc in next*, repeat from * to * around. (24)
Rnd 5: *Sc3, 2sc in next*, repeat from * to * around. (30)
Rnd 6: *Sc4, 2sc in next*, repeat from * to * around. (36)
Rnd 7: *Sc5, 2sc in next*, repeat from * to * around. (42)
Rnd 8: *Sc6, 2sc in next*, repeat from * to * around. (48)
Rnd 9: *Sc7, 2sc in next*, repeat from * to * around. (54)
Rnd 10–Rnd 12: Sc1 in each stitch around. (54)

Rnd 13: With brown sc6, **with pink** sc3, **with brown** sc9, **with pink** sc3, **with brown** sc33. (54)

Rnd 14: With brown sc5, **with pink** sc5, **with brown** sc7, **with pink** sc5, **with brown** sc32. (54)

Rnd 15: With brown sc4, **with pink** sc7, **with brown** sc5, **with pink** sc7, **with brown** sc31. (54)

Rnd 16: With brown sc3, **with pink** sc9, **with brown** sc3, **with pink** sc9, **with brown** sc30. (54)

Rnd 17: With brown sc3, **with pink** sc10, **with brown** sc1, **with pink** sc11, **with brown** sc29. (54)

Rnd 18: With brown sc3, **with pink** sc23, **with brown** sc28. (54)

Rnd 19: With brown sc2tog, sc1, **with pink** sc6, sc2tog, sc7, sc2tog, sc6, **with brown** sc1, *sc2tog, sc7*, repeat from * to * to end. (48)

Rnd 20: With brown sc2tog, sc1, **with pink** sc5, sc2tog, sc6, sc2tog, sc5, **with brown** sc1, *sc2tog, sc6*, repeat from * to * to end. (42)

Rnd 21: With brown sc2tog, sc1, **with pink** sc4, sc2tog, sc5, sc2tog, sc4, **with brown** sc1, *sc2tog, sc5*, repeat from * to * to end. (36)

Rnd 22: With brown sc2tog, sc1, **with pink** sc3, sc2tog, sc4, sc2tog, sc3, **with brown** sc1, *sc2tog, sc4*, repeat from * to * to end. (30)

Rnd 23: With brown sc2tog, sc1, **with pink** sc2, sc2tog, sc3, sc2tog, sc2, **with brown** sc1, *sc2tog, sc3*, repeat from * to * to end. (24)

Rnd 24: With brown sc2tog, sc1, **with pink** sc1, sc2tog, sc2, sc2tog, sc1, **with brown** sc1, *sc2tog, sc2*, repeat from * to * to end. (18)

Attach safety eyes between Rnd 18 and Rnd 19 and stuff the head.

Rnd 25: With brown sc2tog, sc1, **with pink** sc2tog, sc1, sc2tog, **with brown** sc1, *sc2tog, sc1*, repeat from * to * to end. (12)

Cut yarn, close the seam with the brown thread, and weave in the pink thread.

SNOUT

Rnd 1: With pink, start with a magic ring, 6sc in the loop. (6)

Rnd 2: 2sc in each stitch around. (12)

Rnd 3: *Sc1, 2sc in next*, repeat from * to * around. (18)

Rnd 4: *Sc2, 2sc in next*, repeat from * to * around. (24)

Rnd 5: *Sc3, 2sc in next*, repeat from * to * around. (30)

Rnd 6–Rnd 8: Sc1 in each stitch around. (30)

Cut a long thread to attach the snout to the face. Make sure it's centered between the eyes and sew between Rnd 19 and Rnd 25 of the head; when the seam is almost completely sewn, you can stuff the snout and sew it closed.

EARS (MAKE 2)

Rnd 1: With brown, start with a magic ring, 6sc in the loop. (6)

Rnd 2: Sc2, 2dc in each of the next 4 stitches. (10)

Rnd 3: Sc2, 2dc in each of the next 8 stitches. (18)

Cut a long thread and sew the 2sc of Rnd 3 of the ears to Rnd 15–Rnd 17 of the head.

BODY

Rnd 1: With brown ch18, 1dc in third ch from hook, dc14, 3dc in last, continue along other side of chains, dc15, 3dc in last, sl st in first dc. (36)

Rnd 2: Ch2 (doesn't count as first stitch now and throughout), *dc17, 2dc in next*, repeat from * to * one more time, sl st in first dc. (38)

Rnd 3: Ch2, *dc18, 2dc in next*, repeat from * to * one more time, sl st in first dc. (40)

Rnd 4: Ch2, *dc19, 2dc in next*, repeat from * to * one more time, sl st in first dc. (42)

Rnd 5: Ch2, *dc20, 2dc in next*, repeat from * to * one more time, sl st in first dc. (44)

Rnd 6: Ch2, *dc21, 2dc in next*, repeat from * to * one more time, sl st in first dc. (46)

Rnd 7: Ch2, *dc22, 2dc in next*, repeat from * to * one more time, sl st in first dc. (48)

Rnd 8: Ch2, *dc23, 2dc in next*, repeat from * to * one more time, sl st in first dc. (50)

Rnd 9: Ch2, *dc24, 2dc in next*, repeat from * to * one more time, sl st in first dc. (52)

Rnd 10: Ch2, *dc25, 2dc in next*, repeat from * to * one more time, sl st in first dc. (54)

Rnd 11: Ch2, *dc26, 2dc in next*, repeat from * to * one more time, sl st in first dc. (56)

Rnd 12: Ch2, *dc27, 2dc in next*, repeat from * to * one more time, sl st in first dc. (58)

Rnd 13: Ch2, *dc28, 2dc in next*, repeat from * to * one more time, sl st in first dc. (60)

Rnd 14: Ch2, *dc29, 2dc in next*, repeat from * to * one more time, sl st in first dc. (62)

Rnd 15: Ch2, *dc30, 2dc in next*, repeat from * to * one more time, sl st in first dc. (64)

Rnd 16: Ch2, *dc31, 2dc in next*, repeat from * to * one more time, sl st in first dc. (66)

Rnd 17: Ch2, *dc32, 2dc in next*, repeat from * to * one more time, sl st in first dc. (68)

Rnd 18: Ch2, *dc33, 2dc in next*, repeat from * to * one more time, sl st in first dc. (70)

Rnd 19: Ch2, *dc34, 2dc in next*, repeat from * to * one more time, sl st in first dc. (72)

Cut a long tail to close the body in the end. Fold the body in line with the increases to make the belly straight.

ARMS (MAKE 2)

Rnd 1: With brown, start with a magic ring, 6sc in the loop. (6)

Rnd 2: 2sc in each stitch around. (12)

Rnd 3: *Sc1, 2sc in next*, repeat from * to * around. (18)

Rnd 4: *Sc2, 2sc in next*, repeat from * to * around. (24)

Rnd 5–Rnd 9: Sc1 in each stitch around. (24)

Rnd 10: *Sc2, sc2tog*, repeat from * to * around. (18)

Rnd 11–Rnd 12: Sc1 in each stitch around. (18)

Rnd 13: Sl st, ch2 (doesn't count as first stitch now and throughout), dc1 in each stitch around, sl st in first dc. (18)

Rnd 14: Ch2, dc2tog, dc1 in each stitch around, sl st in first dc. (17)

At this point, stuff the hand and, with a piece of brown yarn, sew across the arm between Rnd 12 and Rnd 13.

Rnd 15: Ch2, dc1 in each stitch around, sl st in first dc. (17)

Rnd 16: Ch2, dc2tog, dc1 in each stitch around, sl st in first dc. (16)

Rnd 17: Ch2, dc1 in each stitch around, sl st in first dc. (16)

Rnd 18: Ch2, dc2tog, dc1 in each stitch around, sl st in first dc. (15)

Rnd 19: Ch2, dc1 in each stitch around, sl st in first dc. (15)

Rnd 20: Ch2, dc2tog, dc1 in each stitch around, sl st in first dc. (14)

Rnd 21: Ch2, dc1 in each stitch around, sl st in first dc. (14)

Rnd 22: Ch2, dc2tog, dc1 in each stitch around, sl st in first dc. (13)

Cut a long tail to attach the arms later.

LEGS (MAKE 2)

Rnd 1: With brown, start with a magic ring, ch2 (doesn't count as first stitch now and throughout), 12dc in the loop, sl st in first dc. (12)

Rnd 2: Ch2, *dc1, 2dc in next*, repeat from * to * around, sl st in first dc. (18)

Rnd 3–Rnd 7: Ch2, dc1 in each stitch around, sl st in first dc. (18)

Cut the yarn and weave in the ends.

TAIL

Rnd 1: With brown, start with a magic ring, ch2 (doesn't count as first stitch now and throughout), 6dc in the loop, sl st in first dc. (6)

Rnd 2–Rnd 10: Ch2, dc1 in each stitch around, sl st in first dc. (6)

Cut the yarn and weave in the ends.

PUTTING IT ALL TOGETHER

- Place both legs and the tail between the bottom two layers of the body; use the remaining yarn from the body to sew across the seam, with the legs and tail in between, to close and at the same time attach the parts.
- Sew an arm to each side of the body between Rnd 1 and Rnd 3.
- Sew Rnd 21 of the head to Rnd 1 of the body.

BABY MONKEY

Would you like to share a banana with me?

DIFFICULTY LEVEL

HEAD

Rnd 1: With beige, start with a magic ring, 6sc in the ring. (6)

Rnd 2: 2sc in each stitch around. (12)

Rnd 3: *Sc1, 2sc in next*, repeat from * to * around. (18)

Rnd 4: *Sc2, 2sc in next*, repeat from * to * around. (24)

Rnd 5: *Sc3, 2sc in next*, repeat from * to * around. (30)

Rnd 6: *Sc4, 2sc in next*, repeat from * to * around. (36)

Rnd 7–Rnd 9: Sc1 in each stitch around. (36)

Rnd 10: With beige sc3, **with light pink** sc3, **with beige** sc3, **with light pink** sc3, **with beige** sc24. (36)

Rnd 11: With beige sc2, **with light pink** sc5, **with beige** sc1, **with light pink** sc5, **with beige** sc23. (36)

Rnd 12: With beige sc1, **with light pink** sc13, **with beige** sc22. (36)

Rnd 13: With beige sc1, **with light pink** sc14, **with beige** sc21. (36)

Rnd 14: With beige sc1, **with light pink** sc3, sc2tog, sc4, sc2tog, sc3, **with beige** sc1, sc2tog,*sc4, sc2tog*, repeat from * to * to the end. (30)

Rnd 15: With beige sc1, **with light pink** sc2, *sc2tog, sc3*, repeat from * to * 1 more time, **with beige** sc2tog, *sc3, sc2tog*, repeat from * to * until end. (24)

Rnd 16: With beige sc1, **with light pink** sc1, *sc2tog, sc2*, repeat from * to * 1 more time, sc1, **with beige** sc2tog, sc1, sc2tog, *sc2, sc2tog*, repeat from * to * to end. (18)

At this point, attach the eyes between Rnd 12 and Rnd 13 and fill the head.

Rnd 17: With beige sc1, **with light pink** *sc2tog, sc1*, repeat from * to * 1 more time, sc2tog, **with beige** *sc1, sc2tog*, repeat from * to * until end. (12) Cut the light pink thread and weave in the ends.

Cut a long piece of beige yarn and close the seam; use the remaining thread to attach the head to the body.

SNOUT

Rnd 1: With light pink, start with a magic ring, 6sc in the ring. (6)

Rnd 2: 2sc in each stitch around. (12)

Rnd 3: *Sc3, 2sc in next*, repeat from * to * around. (15)

Rnd 4: Sc1 in each stitch around. (15)

Cut, leaving a long piece of yarn to secure the snout to the face, making sure that the center is exactly between the eyes, and then sew it to Rnd 14 and Rnd 17 of the head. Secure it three-quarters of the way around, fill it up, and then sew it completely shut.

EARS (MAKE 2)

Rnd 1: With beige, start with a magic ring, 6sc in the ring. (6)

Rnd 2: Sc2, 2dc in each of the 4 following stitches, sl st in first sc. (10)

Cut the yarn, leaving a long thread for securing the ears later.

BODY

Rnd 1: With beige ch13, dc1 in third ch from hook, dc9, 3dc in last, continue along other side of chains, dc10, 3dc in last, sl st in first dc. (26)

Rnd 2: Ch2 (from here on does not count as first stitch), *dc12, 2dc in next*, repeat from * to * 1 more time, sl st in first dc. (28)

Rnd 3: Ch2, *dc13, 2dc in next*, repeat from * to * 1 more time, sl st in first dc. (30)

Rnd 4: Ch2, *dc14, 2dc in next*, repeat from * to * 1 more time, sl st in first dc. (32)

Rnd 5: Ch2, *dc15, 2dc in next*, repeat from * to * 1 more time, sl st in first st. (34)

Rnd 6: Ch2, *dc16, 2dc in next*, repeat from * to * 1 more time , sl st in first st. (36)

Rnd 7: Ch2, *dc17, 2dc in next*, repeat from * to * 1 more time, sl st in first dc. (38)

Rnd 8: Ch2, *dc18, 2dc in next*, repeat from * to * 1 more time, sl st in first dc. (40)

Rnd 9: Ch2, *dc19, 2dc in next*, repeat from * to * 1 more time, sl st in first dc. (42)

Rnd 10: Ch2, *dc20, 2dc in next*, repeat from * to * 1 more time, sl st in first dc. (44)

Rnd 11: Ch2, *dc21, 2dc in next*, repeat from * to * 1 more time, sl st in first dc. (46)

Rnd 12: Ch2, *dc22, ch14, dc1 in 3rd ch from hook, dc1 in each of the 11 remaining stitches, 2dc in next stitch on Rnd 11*, repeat from * to * 1 more time, sl st in first dc. Cut a long thread to close the body later.

ARMS (MAKE 2)

Rnd 1: With beige, start with a magic ring, 6sc in the ring. (6)

Rnd 2: 2sc in each stitch around. (12)

Rnd 3: *Sc1, 2sc in next*, repeat from * to * around. (18)

Rnd 4–Rnd 5: Sc1 in each stitch around. (18)

Rnd 6: *Sc1, sc2tog*, repeat from * to * around. (12)

Rnd 7: Sc1 in each stitch around. (12)

Rnd 8: Sl st, ch2 (does not count as first dc from now on), dc1 in each stitch around, sl st in first dc. (12)

Rnd 9: Ch2, dc2tog, dc1 in each stitch around, sl st in first dc. (11)

Now fill up the hand, and then take a piece of yarn and sew along the hand between Rnd 7 and Rnd 8.

Rnd 10: Ch2, dc1 in each stitch around, sl st in first dc. (11)

Rnd 11: Ch2, dc2tog, dc1 in each stitch around, sl st in first dc. (10)

Rnd 12: Ch2, dc1 in each stitch around, sl st in first dc. (10)

Rnd 13: Ch2, dc2tog, dc1 in each stitch around, sl st in first dc. (9)

Cut a long thread for securing the arms later.

TAIL

Rnd 1: With beige, start with a magic ring, ch2 (does not count as the first st for the entire pattern), 6dc in the ring, sl st in first dc. (6)

Rnd 2–Rnd 8: Ch2, dc1 in each stitch around, sl st in first dc. (6)

Cut a long thread to secure the tail later.

PUTTING IT ALL TOGETHER

- Sew the 2 sc from Rnd 2 of an ear to each side of the head between Rnd 12 and Rnd 13.
- Fold the body along the increase lines and use the long yarn left on the body to close the bottom.
- Make a knot in the corners to make the feet.

- Sew an arm on each side of the body between Rnd 1 and Rnd 2.
- Sew the tail against the side of the body at Rnd 11.
- Take the head and sew Rnd 14 onto Rnd 1 of the body.

OWL

Come and hang out with this wise owl.

DIMENSIONS

11.8 in. (30 cm) long and 6.3 in. (16 cm) wide

MATERIALS

DK #3 lightweight yarn (sample shown in Scheepjes Stone Washed):
• white (Moon Stone): 65.6 yd. (60 m)
• beige (Boulder Opal): 142.2 yd. (130 m)
• brown (Brown Agate): 87.5 yd. (80 m)
• orange (Coral): 54.7 yd. (50 m)
Crochet hook: US size D-3 (3 mm)
Gold and black safety eyes, 15 mm
Fiberfill stuffing
Yarn needle and scissors

SPECIAL STITCH

Feather = skip 1 dc, 2dc in next stitch

DIFFICULTY LEVEL

EYES (MAKE 2)

Rnd 1: With white, start with a magic ring, ch2 (doesn't count as first dc now and throughout), dc12 in the loop, sl st 1 in first dc. (12) Don't pull the ring tight, but leave a little hole to insert the eye.

LEFT EYE

Rnd 2: With brown ch1, 2sc in same stitch as ch1, hdc1, (in next stitch: dc3, ch3, sl st in first of 3 ch, 1tr).

RIGHT EYE
Rnd 2: With brown ch6, sl st in fourth ch from hook, dc3 in same stitch as ch6, hdc1, 2sc in next stitch, sl st in same as 2sc.

FOR BOTH EYES
Cut the white and brown yarn to attach the eyes later.

BEAK

Rnd 1: With orange, start with a magic ring. In the ring: ch1, sc1, hdc1, dc1, tr1, dc1, hdc1, sc1, sl st in first sc. Cut the yarn, but leave a long end to sew the beak on later.

HEAD

Rnd 1: With beige, start with a magic ring, sc6 in the ring. (6)
Rnd 2: Sc2 in each stitch around. (12)
Rnd 3: *Sc1, sc2 in next*, repeat from * to * around. (18)
Rnd 4: *Sc2, sc2 in next*, repeat from * to * around. (24)
Rnd 5: *Sc3, sc2 in next*, repeat from * to * around. (30)
Rnd 6: *Sc4, sc2 in next*, repeat from * to * around. (36)
Rnd 7: *Sc5, sc2 in next*, repeat from * to * around. (42)
Rnd 8: *Sc6, sc2 in next*, repeat from * to * around. (48)
Rnd 9: *Sc7, sc2 in next*, repeat from * to * around. (54)
Rnd 10–Rnd 25: Sc1 in each stitch around. (54)
Rnd 26: *Sc7, sc2tog*, repeat from * to * around. (48)
Rnd 27: *Sc6, sc2tog*, repeat from * to * around. (42)
Rnd 28: In back loops only, *sc5, sc2tog*, repeat from * to * around. (36)
Cut a long thread to close the seam of the head later. **Edge: With beige**, attach the yarn in the first unworked front loop of Rnd 27, ch1, sc1 in same stitch as ch1, *skip 2, 7dc in next stitch, skip 2, sc1 in next*, repeat from * to * around, sl st in first sc, cut the yarn and weave in ends. Take the eyes you've just made and insert the safety eyes between Rnd 18 and Rnd 19 (with 5 stitches in between, counted from the white edge) through the head and attach the back of each safety eye inside the head (make extra sure they're firmly attached, since it's a bit harder to attach the back through two layers).
Sew the edges to the head (white part with remaining white yarn and brown piece with the remaining brown yarn).
Sew the beak in the center between the eyes in Rnd 20– Rnd 24.

Stuff the head with fiberfill and close the seam with the remaining yarn.

BODY

Rnd 1: With brown ch18, 1dc in third ch from hook, dc14, 3dc in last, continue along other side of chains, dc15, 3dc in last, sl st in first dc. (36)

Rnd 2: With brown ch2 (doesn't count as first dc now and throughout), dc3, *****with white** feather, **with brown** feather*, repeat from * to * 1 more time, **with white** feather, **with brown** dc4, 2dc in next stitch, dc17, 2dc in next, sl st in first dc. (38)

Rnd 3: With brown ch2, dc5, *****with white** feather, **with brown** feather*, repeat from * to * 1 more time, **with white** feather, **with brown** dc3, 2dc in next stitch, dc18, 2dc in next, sl st in first dc. (40)

Rnd 4: With brown ch2, dc3, *****with white** feather, **with brown** feather*, repeat from * to * 2 more times, **with white** feather, **with brown** dc2, 2dc in next stitch, dc19, 2dc in next, sl st in first dc. (42)

Rnd 5: With brown ch2, dc5, *****with white** feather, **with brown** feather*, repeat from * to * 1 more time, **with white** feather, **with brown** dc5, 2dc in next stitch, dc20, 2dc in next, sl st in first dc. (44)

Rnd 6: With brown ch2, dc3, *****with white** feather, **with brown** feather*, repeat from * to * 2 more times, **with white** feather, **with brown** dc4, 2dc in next stitch, dc21, 2dc in next, sl st in first dc. (46)

Rnd 7: With brown ch2, dc5, *****with white** feather, **with brown** feather*, repeat from * to * 2 more times, **with white** feather, **with brown** dc3, 2dc in next stitch, dc22, 2dc in next, sl st in first dc. (48)

Rnd 8: With brown ch2, dc3, *****with white** feather, **with brown** feather*, repeat from * to * 2 more times, **with white** feather, **with brown** dc6, 2dc in next stitch, dc23, 2dc in next, sl st in first dc. (50)

Rnd 9: With brown ch2, dc5, *****with white** feather, **with brown** feather*, repeat from * to * 2 more times, **with white** feather, **with brown** dc5, 2dc in next stitch, dc24, 2dc in next, sl st in first dc. (52)

Rnd 10: With brown ch2, dc3, *****with white** feather, **with brown** feather*, repeat from * to * 3 more times, **with white** feather, **with brown** dc4, 2dc in next stitch, dc25, 2dc in next, sl st in first dc. (54)

Rnd 11: With brown ch2, dc5, *****with white** feather, **with brown** feather*, repeat from * to * 2 more times, **with white** feather, **with brown** dc7, 2dc in next stitch, dc26, 2dc in next, sl st in first dc. (56)

Rnd 12: With brown ch2, dc3, *****with white** feather, **with brown** feather*, repeat from * to * 3 more times, **with white** feather, **with brown** dc6, 2dc in next stitch, dc27, 2dc in next, sl st in first dc. (58)

Rnd 13: With brown ch2, dc5, ***with white** feather, **with brown** feather*, repeat from * to * 3 more times, **with white** feather, **with brown** dc5, 2dc in next stitch, dc28, 2dc in next, sl st in first dc. (60)

Rnd 14: With brown ch2, dc3, ***with white** feather, **with brown** feather*, repeat from * to * 3 more times, **with white** feather, **with brown** dc8, 2dc in next stitch, dc29, 2dc in next, sl st in first dc. (62)

Rnd 15: With brown ch2, dc5, ***with white** feather, **with brown** feather*, repeat from * to * 3 more times, **with white** feather, **with brown** dc7, 2dc in next stitch, dc30, 2dc in next, sl st in first dc. (64)

Rnd 16: With brown ch2, dc3, ***with white** feather, **with brown** feather*, repeat from * to * 4 more times, **with white** feather, **with brown** dc6, 2dc in next stitch, dc31, 2dc in next, sl st in first dc. (66)

Rnd 17: With brown ch2, dc5, ***with white** feather, **with brown** feather*, repeat from * to * 3 more times, **with white** feather, **with brown** dc9, 2dc in next stitch, dc32, 2dc in next, sl st in first dc. (68)

Rnd 18: With brown ch2, dc3, ***with white** feather, **with brown** feather*, repeat from to * 4 more times, **with white** feather, **with brown** dc8, 2dc in next stitch, dc33, 2dc in next, sl st in first dc. (70)

Rnd 19: With brown ch2, dc5, ***with white** feather, **with brown** feather*, repeat from to * 4 more times, **with white** feather, **with brown** dc7, 2dc in next stitch, dc34, 2dc in next, sl st in first dc. (72)

You can cut the white yarn.

Rnd 20: With brown ch2, *dc35, 2dc in next*, repeat from * to * one more time, sl st in first dc. (74)

Cut the yarn, but leave a long end to close the body in the end; fold the body in line with the increases to make the belly straight.

WINGS (MAKE 2)

Rnd 1: With beige, start with a magic ring, ch2 (doesn't count as first dc now and throughout), 6dc in the ring, sl st in first dc. (6)

Rnd 2: Ch2, 2dc in each stitch around, sl st in first dc. (12)

Rnd 3: Ch2, *dc1, 2dc in next*, repeat from * to * around, sl st in first dc. (18)

Rnd 4: Ch2, *dc2, 2dc in next*, repeat from * to * around, sl st in first dc. (24)

Rnd 5: Ch2, *dc3, 2dc in next*, repeat from * to * around, sl st in first dc. (30)

Rnd 6: Ch2, dc1 in each stitch around, sl st in first dc. (30)

Rnd 7: Ch2, dc2tog twice, dc26, sl st in first dc. (28)

Rnd 8: Ch2, dc2tog twice, dc24, sl st in first dc. (26)

Rnd 9: Ch2, dc2tog twice, dc22, sl st in first dc. (24)

Rnd 10: Ch2, dc2tog twice, dc20, sl st in first dc. (22)

Rnd 11: Ch2, dc2tog twice, dc18, sl st in first dc. (20)

Rnd 12: Ch2, dc2tog twice, dc16, sl st in first dc. (18)
Rnd 13: Ch2, dc2tog twice, dc14, sl st in first dc. (16)
Rnd 14: Ch2, dc2tog twice, dc12, sl st in first dc. (14)
Rnd 15: Ch2, dc2tog twice, dc10, sl st in first dc. (12)
Cut the yarn but leave a long tail to attach the wings in the end.

FEET (MAKE 2)

Rnd 1: With orange, start with a magic ring, 6sc in the ring. (6)
Rnd 2: 2sc in each stitch around. (12)
Rnd 3: *Sc1, 2sc in next*, repeat from * to * around. (18)
Rnd 4: *Sc2, 2sc in next*, repeat from * to * around. (24)
Rnd 5–Rnd 11: Sc1 in each stitch around. (24)
Rnd 12: *Sc1, (in next: 1hdc, 1dc, 1tr, 1dc, 1hdc), sc1, sl st 1*, repeat from * to * around. You'll have three toes (6 repeats).
Cut the yarn but leave a long tail to close the feet in the end.

EARS (MAKE 2)

Rnd 1: With beige, start with a magic ring, ch2 (doesn't count as first dc now and throughout), dc12 in the ring, sl st in first dc. (12)
Rnd 2: Ch2, dc1 in each stitch around, sl st in first dc. (12) Cut the yarn but leave a long tail to sew on the ears in the end.

PUTTING IT ALL TOGETHER

- Sew an ear to each side of the head in Rnd 8.
- Place both feet between the bottom two layers of the body. With the remaining yarn from the body, sew across the seam with the parts in between. This way you close the bottom and assemble the pieces at the same time.
- Stuff the feet lightly. With the remaining yarn, close the seam of the toes by sewing through both layers.
- Sew a wing to each side of the body between Rnd 2 and Rnd 4.
- Finally, sew Rnd 28 of the head to Rnd 1 of the body.

OWLET

Do you want to dive into an adventure with this little owlet?

DIMENSIONS

8.3 in. (21 cm) long and 3.9 in. (10 cm) wide

MATERIALS

DK #3 lightweight yarn (sample shown in Scheepjes Stone Washed):
• white (Moon Stone): 142.2 yd. (130 m)
• beige (Boulder Opal): 76.6 yd. (70 m)
• orange (Coral): 32.8 yd. (30 m)
Crochet hook: US size D-3 (3 mm)
Gold and black safety eyes, 12 mm
Fiberfill stuffing
Yarn needle and scissors

SPECIAL STITCH

Feather = skip 1 dc, 2dc in next stitch

DIFFICULTY LEVEL

EYES (MAKE 2)

Rnd 1: With white, start with a magic ring, 8sc in the ring. (8) Do not overtighten the ring, but leave a hole to insert the eye.

LEFT EYE

Rnd 2: With beige ch1, 2sc in the same stitch as ch, hdc1, (in next stitch: 2dc, ch3, sl st in first of ch3, 1tr).

Rnd 2: With beige ch6, sl st in fourth ch from your hook, 2dc in the same stitch as the ch6, 1hdc, 2sc in the next stitch, sl st in same as 2sc.

FOR BOTH EYES
Cut yarn, leaving long white and beige threads to secure the eyes later.

BEAK

Rnd 1: With orange, start with a magic ring, ch1, 1sc, 1hdc, 1dc, 1tr, 1dc, 1hdc, 1sc, sl st in first sc. (7)
Cut a long thread to secure the beak later.

HEAD

Rnd 1: With white, start with a magic ring, 6sc in the ring.(6)
Rnd 2: 2sc in each sc around. (12)
Rnd 3: *Sc1, 2sc in next*, repeat from * to * around. (18)
Rnd 4: *Sc2, 2sc in next*, repeat from * to * around. (24)
Rnd 5: *Sc3, 2sc in next*, repeat from * to * around. (30)
Rnd 6: *Sc4, 2sc in next*, repeat from * to * around. (36)
Rnd 7: *Sc5, 2sc in next*, repeat from * to * around. (42)
Rnd 8–Rnd 20: Sc1 in each sc around. (42)
Rnd 21: In back loops only, *Sc5, sc2tog*, repeat from * to * around. (36)
Cut a long thread to close the head later.
Edge: With white, attach the thread in the first front loop of Rnd 20 that you have not worked in: ch1, 1sc in same as ch1, *skip 2, 7dc in next, skip 2, sc1 in next*, repeat from * to * around, sl st in first sc.
Cut the thread and weave in the ends.
Take the eyes that you just hooked and insert the safety eyes between Rnd 13 and Rnd 14 (with 6 stitches in between, counted from the white edge) through the head, and attach the back of each safety eye inside the head (check carefully to confirm that they are secure, as it is more difficult to pass them through two layers). Now sew on using the remaining threads of the eye (white piece with white thread and beige piece with beige thread).
Sew the beak between the eyes on Rnd 13–Rnd 18.
Fill the head and close the bottom seam.

BODY

Rnd 1: With white ch13, dc1 in third ch from hook, dc9, 3dc in last, continue along other side of chains, dc10, 3dc in last, sl st in first st. (26)

Rnd 2: With white ch2 (does not count as the first dc for the entire pattern), dc2, **with beige** feather (see Special Stitch on page 77), **with white** feather, **with beige** feather, **with white** dc4, 2dc in next stitch, dc12, 2dc in next, sl st in first dc. (28)

Rnd 3: With white ch2, dc4, **with beige** feather, **with white** feather, **with beige** feather, **with white** dc3, 2dc in next stitch, dc13, 2dc in next, sl st in first dc. (30)

Rnd 4: With white ch2, dc2, *****with beige** feather, **with white** feather *, repeat from * to * 1 more time, **with beige** feather, **with white** dc2, 2dc in next stitch, dc14, 2dc in next, sl st in first dc. (32)

Rnd 5: With white ch2, dc4, **with beige** feather, **with white** feather, **with beige** feather, **with white** dc5, 2dc in next stitch, dc15, 2dc in next, sl st in first dc. (34)

Rnd 6: With white ch2, dc2; *****with beige** feather, **with white** feather *, repeat from * to * 1 more time, **with beige** feather, **with white** dc4, 2dc in next stitch, dc16, 2dc in next, sl st in first dc. (36)

Rnd 7: With white ch2, dc4, *****with beige** feather, **with white** feather*, repeat from * to * 1 more time, **with beige** feather, **with white** dc3, 2dc in next stitch, dc17, 2dc in next, sl st in first dc. (38)

Rnd 8: With white ch2, dc2, *****with beige** feather, **with white** feather*, repeat from * to * 1 more time, **with beige** feather, **with white** dc6, 2dc in next stitch, dc18, 2dc in next, sl st in first dc. (40)

Rnd 9: With white ch2, dc4, *****with beige** feather, **with white** feather*, repeat from * to * 1 more time, **with beige** feather, **with white** dc5, 2dc in next stitch, dc19, 2dc in next, sl st in first dc. (42)

Rnd 10: With white ch2, dc2; *****with beige** feather, **with white** feather*, repeat from * to * 2 more times, **with beige** feather, **with white** dc4, 2dc in next stitch, dc20, 2dc in next, sl st in first dc. (44)

Rnd 11: With white ch2, dc4, *****with beige** feather, **with white** feather*, repeat from * to * 1 more time, **with beige** feather, **with white** dc7, 2dc in next stitch, dc21, 2dc in next, sl st in first dc. (46)

Rnd 12: With white ch2, dc2, *****with beige** feather, **with white** feather*, repeat from * to * 2 more times, **with beige** feather, **with white** dc6, 2dc in next stitch, dc22, 2dc in next, sl st in first dc. (48)

Rnd 13: With white ch2, dc4, *****with beige** feather, **with white** feather*, repeat from * to * 2 more times, **with beige** feather, **with white** dc5, 2dc in next stitch, dc23, 2dc in next, sl st in first dc. (50)

You can cut the beige thread.

Rnd 14: With white ch2, *dc24, 2dc in next*, repeat from * to * 1 more time, sl st in first dc. (52)

Cut a long thread to close the body at the end, fold the body on the line of the increases.

WINGS (MAKE 2)

Rnd 1: With beige, start with a magic ring, ch2 (does not count as the first dc for the entire pattern), 6dc in the ring, sl st in first dc. (6)

Rnd 2: Ch2, 2dc in every stitch around, sl st in first dc. (12)

Rnd 3: Ch2, *dc1, 2dc in next*, repeat from * to * around, sl st in first dc. (18)

Rnd 4: Ch2, *dc2, 2dc in next*, repeat from * to * around, sl st in first dc. (24)

Rnd 5: Ch2, dc1 in each stitch around, sl st in first dc. (24)

Rnd 6: Ch2, dc2tog 3 times, dc18, sl st in first dc. (21)

Rnd 7: Ch2, dc2tog 3 times, dc15, sl st in first dc. (18)

Rnd 8: Ch2, dc2tog 3 times, dc12, sl st in first dc. (15)

Rnd 9: Ch2, dc2tog 3 times, dc9, sl st in first dc. (12)

Rnd 10: Ch2, dc2tog 3 times, dc6, sl st in first dc. (9)

Cut a long thread to secure the wings later.

FEET (MAKE 2)

Rnd 1: With orange, start with a magic ring, 6sc in the ring. (6)

Rnd 2: 2sc in each stitch around. (12)

Rnd 3: *Sc1, 2sc in next*, repeat from * to * around. (18)

Rnd 4–Rnd 5: Sc1 in each stitch around. (18)

Rnd 6: *Sc1, (in next stitch: 1hdc, 1dc, 1tr, 1dc, 1hdc), sl st*, repeat from * to * all around. You will have three toes (6 repeats).

Cut the yarn but leave a long tail to close the feet in the end.

EARS (MAKE 2)

Rnd 1: With beige, start with a magic ring, ch2 (does not count as first dc for the entire pattern), 8dc in the ring, sl st in first dc. (8)

Rnd 2: Ch2, dc1 in each stitch around, sl st in first dc. (8) Cut a long thread for securing the ears later.

PUTTING IT ALL TOGETHER

- Sew on the ears against Rnd 8 of the head.
- Place each foot between the two layers at the bottom of the body, and then use the remaining yarn to sew along the bottom with the two feet in

between, closing the seam and attaching the parts at the same time.

- Fill the feet lightly. With the remaining yarn, sew each foot tightly through both layers of the toes.
- Sew a wing on each side of the body between Rnd 1 and Rnd 3.
- Sew Rnd 21 of the head onto Rnd 1 of the body.

PENGUIN

I'm trying a new way of fishing. Would you like to join me?

DIMENSIONS

11 in. (28 cm) long and 7.1 in. (18 cm) wide

MATERIALS

DK #3 lightweight yarn (sample shown in Scheepjes Stone Washed):
• gray (Smokey Quartz): 164 yd. (150 m)
• white (Moon Stone): 109.4 yd. (100 m)
• orange (Coral): 54.7 yd. (50 m)
Crochet hook: US size D-3 (3 mm)
Black safety eyes, 12 mm
Small amount of fiberfill stuffing
Yarn needle and scissors

DIFFICULTY LEVEL

HEAD

Rnd 1: With gray, start with a magic ring, 6sc in the ring. (6)
Rnd 2: 2sc in each stitch around. (12)
Rnd 3: *Sc1, 2sc in next*, repeat from * to * around. (18)
Rnd 4: *Sc2, 2sc in next*, repeat from * to * around. (24)
Rnd 5: *Sc3, 2sc in next*, repeat from * to * around. (30)
Rnd 6: *Sc4, 2sc in next*, repeat from * to * around. (36)
Rnd 7: *Sc5, 2sc in next*, repeat from * to * around. (42)
Rnd 8: *Sc6, 2sc in next*, repeat from * to * around. (48)
Rnd 9: *Sc7, 2sc in next*, repeat from * to * around. (54)
Rnd 10–Rnd 14: Sc1 in each stitch around. (54)

Rnd 15: Sc6, **with white** sc3, **with gray** sc9, **with white** sc3, **with gray** sc33. (54)

Rnd 16: Sc5, **with white** sc5, **with gray** sc7, **with white** sc5, **with gray** sc32. (54)

Rnd 17: Sc4, **with white** sc7, **with gray** sc5, **with white** sc7, **with gray** sc31. (54)

Rnd 18: Sc3, **with white** sc9, **with gray** sc3, **with white** sc9, **with gray** sc30. (54)

Rnd 19: Sc3, **with white** sc10, **with gray** sc1, **with white** sc11, **with gray** sc29. (54)

Rnd 20: Sc3, **with white** sc23, **with gray** sc28. (54)

Rnd 21: Sc2tog, sc1, **with white** sc6, sc2tog, sc7, sc2tog, sc6, **with gray** sc1, *sc2tog, sc7* repeat from * to * to end. (48)

Rnd 22: Sc2tog, sc1, **with white** sc5, sc2tog, sc6, sc2tog, sc5, **with gray** sc1, *sc2tog, sc6*, repeat from * to * to end. (42)

Rnd 23: Sc2tog, sc1, **with white** sc4, sc2tog, sc5, sc2tog, sc4, **with gray** sc1, *sc2tog, sc5*, repeat from * to * to end. (36)

Rnd 24: Sc2tog, sc1, **with white** sc3, sc2tog, sc4, sc2tog, sc3, **with gray** sc1, *sc2tog, sc4*, repeat from * to * to end. (30)

Rnd 25: Sc2tog, sc1, **with white** sc2, sc2tog, sc3, sc2tog, sc2, **with gray** sc1, *sc2tog, sc3*, repeat from * to * to end. (24)

Rnd 26: Sc2tog, sc1, **with white** sc1, sc2tog, sc2, sc2tog, sc1, **with gray** sc1, *sc2tog, sc2*, repeat from * to * to end. (18)

At this point, attach safety eyes between Rnd 19 and Rnd 20 and stuff the head.

Rnd 27: Sc2tog, sc1, **with white** sc2tog, sc1, sc2tog, **with gray** sc1, *sc2tog, sc1*, repeat from * to * to end. (12)

Cut a long tail and sew the seam closed.

BODY

Rnd 1: With gray ch20, dc in third ch from hook, dc16, 3dc in last, continue along other side of chains, dc17, 3dc in last, sl st in first dc. (40)

Rnd 2: Ch2 (doesn't count as first stitch for entire pattern), *dc19, 2dc in next*, repeat from * to * one more time, sl st in first dc. (42)

Rnd 3: Ch2, *dc20, 2dc in next*, repeat from * to * one more time, sl st in first dc. (44)

Rnd 4: Ch2, *dc21, 2dc in next*, repeat from * to * one more time, sl st in first dc. (46)

Rnd 5: Ch2, *dc22, 2dc in next*, repeat from * to * one more time, sl st in first dc. (48)

Rnd 6: Ch2, *dc23, 2dc in next*, repeat from * to * one more time, sl st in first dc. (50)

Rnd 7: Ch2, *dc24, 2dc in next*, repeat from * to * one more time, sl st in first dc. (52)

Rnd 8: Ch2, *dc25, 2dc in next*, repeat from * to * one more time, sl st in first dc. (54)

Rnd 9: Ch2, *dc26, 2dc in next*, repeat from * to * one more time, sl st in first dc. (56)

Rnd 10: Ch2, dc3, **with white** dc19, **with gray** dc5, 2dc in next, dc27, 2dc in next, sl st in first dc. (58)

Rnd 11: Ch2, dc3, **with white** dc20, **with gray** dc5, 2dc in next, dc28, 2dc in next, sl st in first dc. (60)

Rnd 12: Ch2, dc3, **with white** dc21, **with gray** dc5, 2dc in next, dc29, 2dc in next, sl st in first dc. (62)

Rnd 13: Ch2, dc3, **with white** dc22, **with gray** dc5, 2dc in next, dc30, 2dc in next, sl st in first dc. (64)

Rnd 14: Ch2, dc3, **with white** dc23, **with gray** dc5, 2dc in next, dc31, 2dc in next, sl st in first dc. (66)

Rnd 15: Ch2, dc3, **with white** dc24, **with gray** dc5, 2dc in next, dc32, 2dc in next, sl st in first dc. (68)

Rnd 16: Ch2, dc3, **with white** dc25, **with gray** dc5, 2dc in next, dc33, 2dc in next, sl st in first dc. (70)

Rnd 17: Ch2, dc3, **with white** dc26, **with gray** dc5, 2dc in next, dc34, 2dc in next, sl st in first dc. (72)

Rnd 18: Ch2, dc3, **with white** dc27, **with gray** dc5, 2dc in next, dc35, 2dc in next, sl st in first dc. (74)

Rnd 19: Ch2, dc3, **with white** dc28, **with gray** dc5, 2dc in next, dc36, 2dc in next, sl st in first dc. (76)

Rnd 20: Ch2, dc3, **with white** dc29, **with gray** dc5, 2dc in next, dc37, 2dc in next, sl st in first dc. (78)

Cut a long tail to close body and attach feet in the end.

FEET (MAKE 2)

Rnd 1: With orange, start with a magic ring, 6sc in the ring. (6)

Rnd 2: 2sc in each stitch around. (12)

Rnd 3: *Sc1, 2sc in next*, repeat from * to * around. (18)

Rnd 4: *Sc2, 2sc in next*, repeat from * to * around. (24)

Rnd 5–Rnd 11: Sc1 in each stitch around. (24)

Rnd 12: *Sc1, (in next: hdc1, dc1, tr1, dc1, hdc1), sc1, sl st 1*, repeat around. You'll end up with three toes (6 repeats). Cut a long tail to close the seam of the feet in the end.

WINGS (MAKE 2)

Rnd 1: With gray, start with a magic ring, ch2, 6dc in the ring, sl st in first dc. (6)

Rnd 2: Ch2, 2dc in each stitch around, sl st in first dc. (12)

Rnd 3: Ch2, *dc1, 2dc in next*, repeat from * to * around, sl st in first dc. (18)

Rnd 4: Ch2, *dc2, 2dc in next*, repeat from * to * around, sl st in first dc. (24)

Rnd 5: Ch2, dc1 in each stitch around, sl st in first dc. (24)

Rnd 6: Ch2, *dc2, dc2tog*, repeat from * to * two more times (3 decreases in total), dc12, sl st in first dc. (21)

Rnd 7: Ch2, dc1 in each stitch around, sl st in first dc. (21)

Rnd 8: Ch2, *dc1, dc2tog* repeat two more times (3 decreases in total), dc12, sl st in first dc. (18)

Rnd 9: Ch2, dc1 in each stitch around, sl st in first dc. (18)

Rnd 10: Ch2, dc2tog three times (3 decreases in total), dc12, sl st in first dc. (15)

Rnd 11: Ch2, dc1 in each stitch around, sl st in first dc. (15)

Cut a long tail to attach wings in the end.

BEAK

Rnd 1: With orange, start with a magic ring, 6sc in the ring. (6)

Rnd 2: 2sc in each stitch around. (12)

Rnd 3: *Sc1, 2sc in next*, repeat from * to * around. (18)

Rnd 4–Rnd 5: Sc1 in each stitch around. (18)

Cut a long tail to attach beak in the end.

PUTTING IT ALL TOGETHER

- Place each foot between the bottom two layers of the body; take the remaining yarn from the body and sew across the seam, with the feet in between, to close and at the same time attach the feet.
- Stuff the feet lightly. With the remaining yarn, sew each foot closed, going through both layers of toes.
- Stuff the beak lightly and sew to the head; leave 1 row of white between the beak and the gray point of head.
- Sew Rnd 21 of the head to Rnd 1 of the body.

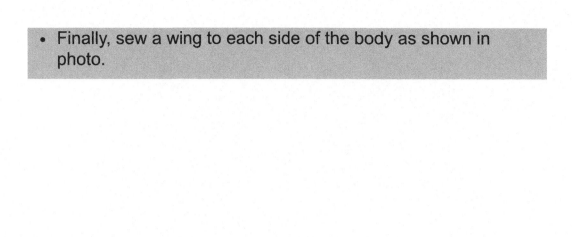

- Finally, sew a wing to each side of the body as shown in photo.

BABY
PENGUIN

Welcome this baby with open arms.

DIMENSIONS

7.1 in. (18 cm) long and 3.9 in. (10 cm) wide

MATERIALS

DK #3 lightweight yarn (sample shown in Scheepjes Stone Washed):
• gray (Smokey Quartz): 142.2 yd. (130 m)
• white (Moon Stone): 76.6 yd. (70 m)
• orange (Coral): 54.7 yd. (50 m)
Crochet hook: US D-3 (3 mm)
Black and blue safety eyes, 12 mm
Small amount of fiberfill stuffing
Yarn needle and scissors

DIFFICULTY LEVEL

HEAD

Rnd 1: With gray, start with a magic ring, 6sc in the ring. (6)
Rnd 2: 2sc in each stitch around. (12)
Rnd 3: *Sc1, 2sc in next*, repeat from * to * around. (18)
Rnd 4: *Sc2, 2sc in next*, repeat from * to * around. (24)
Rnd 5: *Sc3, 2sc in next*, repeat from * to * around. (30)
Rnd 6: *Sc4, 2sc in next*, repeat from * to * around. (36)
Rnd 7– Rnd 9: Sc1 in each stitch around. (36)
Rnd 10: Sc3, **with white** sc3, **with gray** sc3, **with white** sc3, **with gray** sc24. (36)

Rnd 11: Sc2, **with white** sc5, **with gray** sc1, **with white** sc5, **with gray** sc23. (36)

Rnd 12: Sc1, **with white** sc13, **with gray** sc22. (36)

Rnd 13: Sc1, **with white** sc14, **with gray** sc21. (36)

Rnd 14: Sc1, **with white** sc3, sc2tog, sc4, sc2tog, sc3, **with gray** sc1, sc2tog, *sc4, sc2tog*, repeat from * to * to end. (30)

Rnd 15: Sc1, **with white** sc2, *sc2tog, sc3*, repeat from * to * 1 more time, **with gray** sc2tog, *sc3, sc2tog*, repeat from * to * to end. (24)

Rnd 16: Sc1, **with white** sc1, *sc2tog, sc2*, repeat from * to * 1 more time, sc1, **with gray** sc2tog, sc1, sc2tog, *sc2, sc2tog*, repeat from * to * to end. (18)

At this point, attach safety eyes between Rnd 12 and Rnd 13 and stuff the head.

Rnd 17: Sc1, **with white** *sc2tog, sc1*, repeat from * to * one more time, sc2tog, **with gray** *sc1, sc2tog*, repeat from * to * to end. (12)

Cut white yarn and weave it in. Cut a long tail of the gray yarn and sew the seam closed; you can use the remaining yarn to attach head to body later.

BODY

Rnd 1: With gray ch13, 1dc in third ch from hook, dc9, 4dc in last, continue along other side of chains, dc9, 3dc in last, sl st in first dc. (26)

Rnd 2: Ch2 (doesn't count as first stitch for entire pattern) *dc12, 2dc in next*, repeat from * to * one more time, sl st in first dc. (28)

Rnd 3: Ch2, *dc13, 2dc in next*, repeat from * to * one more time, sl st in first dc. (30)

Rnd 4: Ch2, dc3, **with white** dc8, **with gray** dc3, 2dc in next, dc14, 2dc in next, sl st in first dc. (32)

Rnd 5: Ch2, dc3, **with white** dc9, **with gray** dc3, 2dc in next, dc15, 2dc in next, sl st in first dc. (34)

Rnd 6: Ch2, dc3, **with white** dc10, **with gray** dc3, 2dc in next, dc16, 2dc in next, sl st in first dc. (36)

Rnd 7: Ch2, dc3, **with white** dc11, **with gray** dc3, 2dc in next, dc17, 2dc in next, sl st in first dc. (38)

Rnd 8: Ch2, dc3, **with white** dc12, **with gray** dc3, 2dc in next, dc18, 2dc in next, sl st in first dc. (40)

Rnd 9: Ch2, dc3, **with white** dc13, **with gray** dc3, 2dc in next, dc19, 2dc in next, sl st in first dc. (42)

Rnd 10: Ch2, dc3, **with white** dc14, **with gray** dc3, 2dc in next, dc20, 2dc in next, sl st in first dc. (44)

Rnd 11: Ch2, dc3, **with white** dc15, **with gray** dc3, 2dc in next, dc21, 2dc in next, sl st in first dc. (46)

You can cut the white yarn and weave it in.

Rnd 12: Ch2, *dc22, 2dc in next*, repeat from * to * one more time, sl st in first dc. (48)

Cut a long tail to close the body and attach feet at the end, making sure to fold the body on the line of the increases.

FEET (MAKE 2)

Rnd 1: With orange, start with a magic ring, 6sc in the ring. (6)

Rnd 2: 2sc in each stitch around. (12)

Rnd 3: *Sc1, 2sc in next*, repeat from * to * around. (18)

Rnd 4–Rnd 5: Sc1 in each stitch around. (18)

Rnd 6: *Sc1, (in next: hdc1, dc1, tr1, dc1, hdc1), sl st 1*, repeat around. You'll end up with three toes (6 repeats). Cut a long tail to close the seam of the feet at the end.

WINGS (MAKE 2)

Rnd 1: With gray, start with a magic ring, ch2, 6dc in the ring, sl st in first dc. (6)

Rnd 2: Ch2, 2dc in each stitch around, sl st in first dc. (12)

Rnd 3: Ch2, *dc1, 2dc in next*, repeat from * to * around, sl st in first dc. (18)

Rnd 4: Ch2, dc1 in each stitch around, sl st in first dc. (18)

Rnd 5: Ch2, *dc1, dc2tog*, repeat from * to * two more times (3 decreases in total), dc9, sl st in first dc. (15)

Rnd 6: Ch2, dc1 in each stitch around, sl st in first dc. (15)

Rnd 7: Ch2, dc2tog three times (3 decreases in total), dc9, sl st in first dc. (12)

Rnd 8: Ch2, dc1 in each stitch around, sl st in first dc. (12)

Cut a long tail to attach wings at the end.

BEAK

Rnd 1: With orange, start with a magic ring, 6sc in the ring. (6)

Rnd 2: 2sc in each stitch around. (12)

Rnd 3: Sc1 in each stitch around. (12)

Cut a long tail to attach the beak at the end.

PUTTING IT ALL TOGETHER

- Place the feet between the bottom two layers of the body. Using the remaining yarn from the body, sew across the seam, with the feet in between, closing the body and at the same time attaching the feet.

- Stuff the feet lightly. With the remaining yarn, sew each foot closed going through both layers of toes.
- Stuff the beak very lightly and sew to the head, in between the eyes.
- Sew a wing to each side of the body in Rnd 1–Rnd 3.
- Sew Rnd 14 of the head to Rnd 1 of the body.

SHEEP

DIMENSIONS

12.6 in. (32 cm) long and 5.9 in. (15 cm) wide

MATERIALS

DK #3 lightweight yarn (sample shown in Scheepjes Stone Washed):
• gray (Smokey Quartz): 196.9 yd. (180 m)
• white (Moon Stone): 87.5 yd. (80 m)
Crochet hook: US D-3 (3 mm)
Black and blue safety eyes, 15 mm Fiberfill stuffing
Yarn needle and scissors

DIFFICULTY LEVEL

HEAD

Rnd 1: With gray, start with a magic ring, 6sc in the ring. (6)
Rnd 2: 2sc in each stitch around. (12)
Rnd 3: *Dc3tog in 1 stitch, 2sc in next*, repeat from * to * around. (18)
Note: The dc3tog bobbles tend to pop to the inside, so I like to pop them all out with my finger after each round.
Rnd 4: *2sc in next, sc1, dc3tog in 1 stitch*, repeat from * to * around. (24)
Rnd 5: *2sc in next, dc3tog in 1 stitch, sc2*, repeat from * to * around. (30)
Rnd 6: *2sc in next, dc3tog in 1 stitch, sc2, dc3tog in 1 stitch*, repeat from * to * around. (36)
Rnd 7: *2sc in next, dc3tog in 1 stitch, sc2, dc3tog in 1 stitch, sc1*, repeat from * to * around. (42)
Rnd 8: *2sc in next, dc3tog in 1 stitch, sc2, dc3tog in 1 stitch, sc2*, repeat from * to * around. (48)

Rnd 9: *2sc in next, dc3tog in 1 stitch, sc2, dc3tog in 1 stitch, sc2, dc3tog in 1 stitch*, repeat from * to * around. (54)

Rnd 10: *Sc1, dc3tog in next stitch, sc1*, repeat from * to * around. (54)

Rnd 11: *Dc3tog in next stitch, sc2*, repeat from * to * around. (54)

Rnd 12: *Sc2, dc3tog in next stitch*, repeat from * to * around. (54)

Rnd 13–Rnd 15: Repeat Rnd 10–Rnd 12.

Rnd 16–Rnd 30: Continue with white, sc1 in each stitch around. (54)

Rnd 31: *Sc7, sc2tog*, repeat from * to * around. (48)

Rnd 32: *Sc6, sc2tog*, repeat from * to * around. (42)

Rnd 33: *Sc5, sc2tog*, repeat from * to * around. (36)

Rnd 34: *Sc4, sc2tog*, repeat from * to * around. (30)

Rnd 35: *Sc3, sc2tog*, repeat from * to * around. (24)

Rnd 36: *Sc2, sc2tog*, repeat from * to * around. (18) Now attach the eyes between Rnd 21 and Rnd 22 with 12 stitches between them and stuff the head.

Rnd 37: *Sc1, sc2tog* repeat from * to * around. (12)

Cut yarn, weave through the 12 remaining stitches, pull tight and secure.

EARS (MAKE 2)

Rnd 1: With gray, start with a magic ring, 6sc in the ring. (6)

Rnd 2: 2sc in each stitch around. (12)

Rnd 3: *Sc1, 2sc in next*, repeat from * to * around. (18)

Rnd 4–Rnd 7: Sc1 in each stitch around. (18)

Rnd 8: *Sc1, sc2tog*, repeat from * to * around. (12)

Rnd 9: Sc2tog, sc1 in each stitch around. (11)

Rnd 10: Sc2tog, sc1 in each stitch around. (10)

Rnd 11: Sc2tog, sc1 in each stitch around. (9)

Rnd 12: Sc2tog, sc1 in each stitch around. (8)

Cut yarn but leave a long tail and sew ears to head in Rnd 15.

BODY

Rnd 1: With gray ch18, 1dc in third ch from hook, dc14, 3dc in last, continue along other side of chains, dc15, 3dc in last, sl st in first dc. (36)

Rnd 2: Ch2 (doesn't count as first stitch now and throughout), *dc17, 2dc in next*, repeat from * to * one more time, sl st in first dc. (38)

Rnd 3: Ch2, *dc18, 2dc in next*, repeat from * to * one more time, sl st in first dc. (40)

Rnd 4: Ch2, *dc19, 2dc in next*, repeat from * to * one more time, sl st in first dc. (42)

Rnd 5: Ch2, *dc20, 2dc in next*, repeat from * to * one more time, sl st in first dc. (44)

Rnd 6: Ch2, *dc21, 2dc in next*, repeat from * to * one more time, sl st in first dc. (46)

Rnd 7: Ch2, *dc22, 2dc in next*, repeat from * to * one more time, sl st in first dc. (48)

Rnd 8: Ch2, *dc23, 2dc in next*, repeat from * to * one more time, sl st in first dc. (50)

Rnd 9: Ch2, *dc24, 2dc in next*, repeat from * to * one more time, sl st in first dc. (52)

Rnd 10: Ch2, *dc25, 2dc in next*, repeat from * to * one more time, sl st in first dc. (54)

Rnd 11: Ch2, *dc26, 2dc in next*, repeat from * to * one more time, sl st in first dc. (56)

Rnd 12: Ch2, *dc27, 2dc in next*, repeat from * to * one more time, sl st in first dc. (58)

Rnd 13: Ch2, *dc28, 2dc in next*, repeat from * to * one more time, sl st in first dc. (60)

Rnd 14: Ch2, *dc29, 2dc in next*, repeat from * to * one more time, sl st in first dc. (62)

Rnd 15: Ch2, *dc30, 2dc in next*, repeat from * to * one more time, sl st in first dc. (64)

Rnd 16: Ch2, *dc31, 2dc in next*, repeat from * to * one more time, sl st in first dc. (66)

Rnd 17: Ch2, *dc32, 2dc in next*, repeat from * to * one more time, sl st in first dc. (68)

Rnd 18: Ch2, *dc33, 2dc in next*, repeat from * to * one more time, sl st in first dc. (70)

Rnd 19: Ch2, *dc34, 2dc in next*, repeat from * to * one more time, sl st in first dc. (72)

Cut a long tail to close the body in the end; fold the body in line with the increases to make the belly straight.

ARMS (MAKE 2)

Rnd 1: With gray, start with a magic ring, 6sc in the ring. (6)
Rnd 2: 2sc in each stitch around. (12)
Rnd 3: *Sc1, 2sc in next*, repeat from * to * around. (18)
Rnd 4: *Sc2, 2sc in next*, repeat from * to * around. (24)
Rnd 5–Rnd 9: Sc1 in each stitch around. (24)
Rnd 10: *Sc2, sc2tog*, repeat from * to * around. (18)

Rnd 11–Rnd 12: Sc1 in each stitch around. (18)

Rnd 13: Sl st 1, ch2 (doesn't count as first stitch now and throughout), dc1 in each stitch around, sl st in first dc. (18)

Rnd 14: Ch2, dc2tog, dc1 in each stitch around, sl st in first dc. (17)

At this point, stuff the hand and, with a small piece of the blue yarn, sew across the arm between Rnd 12 and Rnd 13.

Rnd 15: Ch2, dc1 in each stitch around, sl st in first dc. (17)

Rnd 16: Ch2, dc2tog, dc1 in each stitch around, sl st in first dc. (16)

Rnd 17: Ch2, dc1 in each stitch around, sl st in first dc. (16)

Rnd 18: Ch2, dc2tog, dc1 in each stitch around, sl st in first dc. (15)

Rnd 19: Ch2, dc1 in each stitch around, sl st in first dc. (15)

Rnd 20: Ch2, dc2tog, dc1 in each stitch around, sl st in first dc. (14)

Rnd 21: Ch2, dc1 in each stitch around, sl st in first dc. (14)

Rnd 22: Ch2, dc2tog, dc1 in each stitch around, sl st in first dc. (13)

Cut a long tail to attach arms to body later.

LEGS (MAKE 2)

Rnd 1: With gray, start with a magic ring, ch2, 12dc in the ring, sl st in first dc. (12)

Rnd 2: Ch2, *dc1, 2dc in next*, repeat from * to * around, sl st in first dc. (18)

Rnd 3–Rnd 7: Ch2, dc1 in each stitch around, sl st in first dc. (18)

Cut yarn and weave in ends.

PUTTING IT ALL TOGETHER

- Place both legs between the bottom two layers of the body, and, with the remaining yarn from the body, sew across the seam, with the legs in between, to close the body and at the same time attach the legs.
- Sew an arm to each side of the body between Rnd 1 and Rnd 3.
- Sew Rnd 24 of the head (ears not included) to Rnd 1 of the body.

LAMB

Will you be this lamb's friend?

DIMENSIONS

6.7 in. (17 cm) long and 3.9 in. (10 cm) wide

MATERIALS

DK #3 lightweight yarn (sample shown in Scheepjes Stone Washed):
• white (Moon Stone): 54.7 yd. (50 m)
• light gray (Crystal Quartz): 109.4 yd. (100 m)
Crochet hook: US D-3 (3 mm)
Black and blue safety eyes, 12 mm
Fiberfill stuffing
Yarn needle and scissors

DIFFICULTY LEVEL

HEAD

Rnd 1: With gray, start with a magic ring, 6sc in the ring. (6)
Rnd 2: 2sc in each stitch around. (12)
Rnd 3: *Dc3tog in 1 stitch, 2sc in next*, repeat from * to * around. (18)
Note: The dc3tog bobbles tend to pop to the inside, so I like to pop them out with my finger after each round.
Rnd 4: *2sc in next, sc1, dc3tog in 1 stitch*, repeat from * to * around. (24)
Rnd 5: *2sc in next, sc1, dc3tog in 1 stitch, sc1*, repeat from * to * around. (30)
Rnd 6: *2sc in next, dc3tog in 1 stitch, sc2, dc3tog in 1 stitch*, repeat from * to * around. (36)
Rnd 7: *Sc1, dc3tog in next stitch, sc1*, repeat from * to * around. (36)
Rnd 8: *Dc3tog in next stitch, sc2*, repeat from * to * around. (36)

Rnd 9: *Sc2, dc3tog in next stitch*, repeat from * to * around. (36)
Rnd 10–Rnd 17: Continue with white, sc1 in each stitch around. (36)
Rnd 18: *Sc4, sc2tog*, repeat from * to * around. (30)
Rnd 19: *Sc3, sc2tog*, repeat from * to * around. (24)
Rnd 20: *Sc2, sc2tog*, repeat from * to * around. (18) Now attach the eyes between Rnd 12 and Rnd 13 with 7 stitches between them and stuff the head.
Rnd 21: *Sc1, sc2tog*, repeat from * to * around. (12)
Cut the yarn, weave through the 12 remaining stitches, pull tight, and secure, but leave a long tail to attach it to the body later.

EARS (MAKE 2)

Rnd 1: With gray, start with a magic ring, 6sc in the ring. (6)
Rnd 2: 2sc in each stitch around. (12)
Rnd 3–Rnd 4: Sc1 in each stitch around. (12)
Rnd 5: *Sc1, sc2tog*, repeat from * to * around. (8)
Rnd 6–Rnd 9: Sc1 in each stitch around. (8)
Cut yarn but leave a long tail and sew the ears to the head in Rnd 9.

BODY

Rnd 1: With gray ch13, 1dc in 3rd ch from hook, dc9, 3dc in last, continue along other side of chains, dc9, 4dc in last, sl st in first dc. (26)
Rnd 2: Ch2 (doesn't count as first stitch now and throughout), *dc12, 2dc in next*, repeat from * to * one more time, sl st in first dc. (28)
Rnd 3: Ch2, *dc13, 2dc in next*, repeat from * to * one more time, sl st in first dc. (30)
Rnd 4: Ch2, *dc14, 2dc in next*, repeat from * to * one more time, sl st in first dc. (32)
Rnd 5: Ch2, *dc15, 2dc in next*, repeat from * to * one more time, sl st in first dc. (34)
Rnd 6: Ch2, *dc16, 2dc in next*, repeat from * to * one more time, sl st in first dc. (36)
Rnd 7: Ch2, *dc17, 2dc in next*, repeat from * to * one more time, sl st in first dc. (38)
Rnd 8: Ch2, *dc18, 2dc in next*, repeat from * to * one more time, sl st in first dc. (40)
Rnd 9: Ch2, *dc19, 2dc in next*, repeat from * to * one more time, sl st in first dc. (42)
Rnd 10: Ch2, *dc20, 2dc in next*, repeat from * to * one more time, sl st in first dc. (44)

Rnd 11: Ch2, *dc21, 2dc in next*, repeat from * to * one more time, sl st in first dc. (46)

Rnd 12: Ch2, *dc22, ch14, 1dc in third ch from hook, 1dc in each of the 11 remaining chains, 2dc in next stitch of Rnd 11*, repeat from * to * one more time, sl st in first dc.

Cut a long tail to close the body.

ARMS (MAKE 2)

Rnd 1: With gray, start with a magic ring, 6sc in the ring. (6)

Rnd 2: 2sc in each stitch around. (12)

Rnd 3: *Sc1, 2sc in next*, repeat from * to * around. (18)

Rnd 4–Rnd 5: Sc1 in each stitch around. (18)

Rnd 6: *Sc1, sc2tog*, repeat from * to * around. (12)

Rnd 7: Sc1 in each stitch around. (12)

Rnd 8: Sl st 1, ch2 (doesn't count as first stitch now and throughout), dc1 in each stitch around, sl st in first dc. (12)

Rnd 9: Ch2, dc2tog, dc1 in each stitch around, sl st in first dc. (11)

At this point, stuff the hand and use a small piece of the gray yarn to sew across the arm between Rnd 7 and Rnd 8.

Rnd 10: Ch2, dc1 in each stitch around, sl st in first dc. (11)

Rnd 11: Ch2, dc2tog, dc1 in each stitch around, sl st in first dc. (10)

Rnd 12: Ch2, dc1 in each stitch around, sl st in first dc. (10)

Rnd 13: Ch2, dc2tog, dc1 in each stitch around, sl st in first dc. (9)

Cut a long tail for attaching the arms.

PUTTING IT ALL TOGETHER

- Fold the body in line with the increases to make the belly straight and sew closed.
- Tie a knot in the corners to form the feet.
- Sew the back of Rnd 18 of the head to Rnd 1 of the body.
- Sew an arm on each side of the body between Rnd 1 and Rnd 2.

OTHER ANIMALS
AND FRIENDS

CALICO CAT

This yarn kitten loves yarn.

MATERIALS

DK #3 lightweight yarn (sample shown in Scheepjes Stone Washed):
• black (Black Onyx): 142.2 yd. (130 m)
• white (Moon Stone): 142.2 yd. (130 m)
• yellow (Yellow Jasper): 142.2 yd. (130 m)
Tiny bit of light pink yarn for nose
Crochet hook: US size D-3 (3 mm)
Brown and black safety eyes, 15 mm
Small amount of fiberfill stuffing
Yarn needle and scissors

DIFFICULTY LEVEL

FIRST EAR

Rnd 1: With yellow, start with a magic ring, 6sc in the ring. (6)
Rnd 2: Sc1 in each stitch around. (6)
Rnd 3: 2sc in each stitch around. (12)
Rnd 4–Rnd 5: Sc1 in each stitch around. (12)
Rnd 6: *Sc1, 2sc in next*, repeat from * to * around. (18)
Rnd 7–Rnd 8: Sc1 in each stitch around. (18)
Cut yarn and weave in ends.

SECOND EAR

Rnd 1: With black, start with a magic ring, 6sc in the ring. (6)
Rnd 2: Sc1 in each stitch around. (6)
Rnd 3: 2sc in each stitch around. (12)
Rnd 4–Rnd 5: Sc1 in each stitch around. (12)
Rnd 6: *Sc1, 2sc in next*, repeat from * to * around. (18)
Rnd 7–Rnd 8: Sc1 in each stitch around. (18)
Don't cut the yarn!

HEAD

Rnd 1: Continue with the black yarn from the second ear, ch9, **take first ear**, sc in each of the 18 stitches of first ear, sc in each of the 9 chains you just made, sc in each of the 18 stitches of second ear. (54)

Rnd 2: Sc13, **with white** sc9, **with black** sc32. (54)

Rnd 3: Sc11, **with white** sc13, **with black** sc30. (54)

Rnd 4: Sc9, **with white** sc17, **with black** sc28. (54)

Rnd 5: Sc7, **with white** sc21, **with black** sc26. (54)

Rnd 6: Sc6, **with white** sc24, **with black** sc24. (54)

Rnd 7: Sc5, **with white** sc27, **with black** sc22. (54)

Rnd 8: Sc4, **with white** sc30, **with black** sc20. (54)

Rnd 9: Sc3, **with white** sc33, **with black** sc18. (54)

Rnd 10: Sc2, **with white** sc36, **with black** sc16. (54)

Rnd 11: Sc1, **with white** sc39, **with black** sc14. (54)

Rnd 12: With white *sc7, sc2tog*, repeat from * to * 3 more times, sc6, **with black** sc1, sc2tog, sc7, sc2tog. (48)

Rnd 13: With white *sc6, sc2tog*, repeat from * to * 4 more times, **with black** sc6, sc2tog. (42)

Rnd 14: With white *sc5, sc2tog*, repeat from * to * 4 more times, **with black** sc5, sc2tog. (36)

Rnd 15: With white *sc4, sc2tog*, repeat from * to * 4 more times, **with black** sc4, sc2tog. (30)

Rnd 16: With white *sc3, sc2tog*, repeat from * to * 4 more times, **with black** sc3, sc2tog. (24)

Rnd 17: With white *sc2, sc2tog*, repeat from * to * 4 more times, **with black** sc2, sc2tog. (18)

At this point, attach the safety eyes between Rnd 9 and Rnd 10 of head; stuff the head.

Rnd 18: With white *sc1, sc2tog*, repeat from * to * 4 more times, **with black** sc1, sc2tog. (12)

Fold seam flat and sew the front and the back of the head together; weave in ends.

Embroider the nose with light pink yarn at Rnd 12 and Rnd 13, centered between the eyes.

BODY

Rnd 1: With black ch20, dc in third ch from hook, dc16, 3dc in last, continue along other side of chains, dc17, 3dc in last, sl st in first dc. (40)

Rnd 2: Ch2 (doesn't count as first stitch for entire pattern), *dc19, 2dc in next*, repeat from * to * one more time, sl st in first dc. (42)

Rnd 3: Ch2, dc3, **with white** dc12, **with black** dc5, 2dc in next, dc20, 2dc in next, sl st in first dc. (44)

Rnd 4: Ch2, dc3, **with white** dc13, **with black** dc5, 2dc in next, dc21, 2dc in next, sl st in first dc. (46)

Rnd 5: Ch2, dc3, **with white** dc14, **with black** dc5, 2dc in next, dc22, 2dc in next, sl st in first dc. (48)

Rnd 6: Ch2, dc3, **with white** dc15, **with black** dc5, 2dc in next, dc23, 2dc in next, sl st in first dc. (50)

Rnd 7: Ch2, dc3, **with white** dc16, **with black** dc5, 2dc in next, dc24, 2dc in next, sl st in first dc. (52)

Rnd 8: Ch2, dc3, **with white** dc17, **with black** dc5, 2dc in next, dc25, 2dc in next, sl st in first dc. (54)

Rnd 9: Ch2, dc3, **with white** dc18, **with black** dc5, 2dc in next, dc26, 2dc in next, sl st in first dc. (56)

Rnd 10: Ch2, dc3, **with white** dc19, **with black** dc5, 2dc in next, dc27, 2dc in next, sl st in first dc. (58)

Rnd 11: Ch2, dc3, **with white** dc20, **with black** dc5, 2dc in next, dc28, 2dc in next, sl st in first dc. (60)

Rnd 12: Ch2, dc3, **with white** dc21, **with black** dc5, 2dc in next, dc29, 2dc in next, sl st in first dc. (62)

Rnd 13: Ch2, dc4, **with white** dc20, **with black** dc6, 2dc in next, dc30, 2dc in next, sl st in first dc. (64)

Rnd 14: Ch2, dc5, **with white** dc19, **with black** dc7, 2dc in next, dc31, 2dc in next, sl st in first dc. (66)

You can cut the black yarn and weave it in.

Rnd 15: With yellow ch2, dc6, **with white** dc18, **with yellow** dc8, 2dc in next, dc32, 2dc in next, sl st in first dc. (68)

Rnd 16: Ch2, dc7, **with white** dc17, **with yellow** dc9, 2dc in next, dc33, 2dc in next, sl st in first dc. (70)

Rnd 17: Ch2, dc8, **with white** dc16, **with yellow** dc10, 2dc in next, dc34, 2dc in next, sl st in first dc. (72)

Rnd 18: Ch2, dc9, **with white** dc15, **with yellow** dc11, 2dc in next, dc35, 2dc in next, sl st in first dc. (74)

Rnd 19: Ch2, *dc36, 2dc in next*, repeat from * to * one more time, sl st in first dc. (76)

Rnd 20: Ch2, *dc37, 2dc in next*, repeat from * to * one more time, sl st in first dc. (78)

Cut a long tail to close body and attach feet in the end.

ARMS (MAKE 2)

Rnd 1: With white, start with a magic ring, 6sc in the ring. (6)

Rnd 2: 2sc in each stitch around. (12)

Rnd 3: *Sc1, 2sc in next*, repeat from * to * around. (18)

Rnd 4: *Sc2, 2sc in next*, repeat from * to * around. (24)

Rnd 5–Rnd 9: Sc1 in each stitch around. (24)

Rnd 10: *Sc2, sc2tog*, repeat from * to * around. (18)

Rnd 11–Rnd 12: Sc1 in each stitch around. (18)

Cut a long white tail to use after Rnd 14.

Rnd 13: With black sl st 1, ch2, dc1 in each stitch around, sl st in first dc. (18)

Rnd 14: Ch2, dc2tog, dc1 in each stitch around, sl st in first dc. (17)

At this point, stuff the hand (not too much) and sew across the arm between Rnd 12 and Rnd 13.

Rnd 15: Ch2, dc1 in each stitch around, sl st in first dc. (17)

Rnd 16: Ch2, dc2tog, dc1 in each stitch around, sl st in first dc. (16)

Rnd 17: Ch2, dc1 in each stitch around, sl st in first dc. (16)

Rnd 18: Ch2, dc2tog, dc1 in each stitch around, sl st in first dc. (15)

Rnd 19: Ch2, dc1 in each stitch around, sl st in first dc. (15)

Rnd 20: Ch2, dc2tog, dc1 in each stitch around, sl st in first dc. (14)

Rnd 21: Ch2, dc1 in each stitch around, sl st in first dc. (14)

Rnd 22: Ch2, dc2tog, dc1 in each stitch around, sl st in first dc. (13)

Cut a long tail to attach the arms to the body in the end.

LEGS (MAKE 2)

Rnd 1: With white, start with a magic ring, 6sc in the ring. (6)

Rnd 2: 2sc in each stitch around. (12)

Rnd 3: *Sc1, 2sc in next*, repeat from * to * around. (18)

Rnd 4: *Sc2, 2sc in next*, repeat from * to * around. (24)

Rnd 5–Rnd 9: Sc1 in each stitch around. (24)

Rnd 10: *Sc2, sc2tog*, repeat from * to * around. (18)

Rnd 11–Rnd 12: Sc1 in each stitch around. (18)

Cut a long white tail to use after Rnd 14.

Rnd 13: With yellow sl st 1, ch2, dc1 in each stitch around, sl st in first dc. (18)

Rnd 14: Ch2, dc2tog, dc1 in each stitch around, sl st in first dc. (17)

At this point, stuff the foot (not too much) and sew across the leg between Rnd 12 and Rnd 13.

Rnd 15: Ch2, dc1 in each stitch around, sl st in first dc. (17)

Rnd 16: Ch2, dc2tog, dc1 in each stitch around, sl st in first dc. (16)

Rnd 17: Ch2, dc1 in each stitch around, sl st in first dc. (16)

Rnd 18: Ch2, dc2tog, dc1 in each stitch around, sl st in first dc. (15)

Cut the yarn and weave in ends.

TAIL

Rnd 1: With yellow, start with a magic ring, 6sc in the ring. (6)

Rnd 2: 2sc in each stitch around. (12)

Rnd 3–Rnd 30: Sc1 in each stitch around. (12)

Stuff the tail every few rounds while you crochet the tail. Cut the yarn and weave in the ends.

PUTTING IT ALL TOGETHER

- Sew Rnd 14 of the head (not counting ears) to Rnd 1 of the body.
- Place both legs and the tail between the bottom two layers of the body and use the remaining yarn from the body to sew across the seam to close the body and at the same time attach all parts.
- Sew an arm to each side of the body between Rnd 2 and Rnd 4.

ELEPHANT

Join the circus with me!

DIMENSIONS

13.4 in. (34 cm) long and 6.3 in. (16 cm) wide

MATERIALS

DK #3 lightweight yarn (sample shown in Scheepjes Stone Washed):
• blue (Blue Apatite): 284.3 yd. (260 m)
Crochet hook: US size D-3 (3 mm)
Black safety eyes, 12 mm
Fiberfill stuffing
Yarn needle and scissors

DIFFICULTY LEVEL

EARS (MAKE 2)

Rnd 1: Start with a magic ring, 6sc in the ring. (6)
Rnd 2: 2sc in each stitch around. (12)
Rnd 3: *Sc1, 2sc in next*, repeat from * to * around. (18)
Rnd 4: *Sc2, 2sc in next*, repeat from * to * around. (24)
Rnd 5: *Sc3, 2sc in next*, repeat from * to * around. (30)
Rnd 6: *Sc4, 2sc in next*, repeat from * to * around. (36)
Rnd 7: *Sc5, 2sc in next*, repeat from * to * around. (42)
Rnd 8–Rnd 17: Sc1 in each stitch around. (42)
Rnd 18: Sc6, *sc2tog, sc4*, repeat from * to * 5 more times. (36)
Rnd 19: Sc6, *sc2tog, sc3*, repeat from * to * 5 more times. (30)
Rnd 20: Sc6, *sc2tog, sc2*, repeat from * to * 5 more times. (24)

Cut yarn of first ear. When finished with the second ear, don't cut the yarn—continue with the head instructions. Fold first ear flat after the next 3 stitches (in the center of the 6 stitches that haven't been decreased).

HEAD

Rnd 1: In second ear sc3, take the first ear and continue in the stitch after the point you folded it, sc24, continue in second ear, sc21. (48)

Rnd 2: *Sc7, 2sc in next*, repeat from * to * around. (54)

Rnd 3–Rnd 7: Sc1 in each stitch around. (54)

Rnd 8: *Sc7, sc2tog*, repeat from * to * around. (48)

Rnd 9: Sc1 in each stitch around. (48)

Rnd 10: *Sc6, sc2tog*, repeat from * to * around. (42)

Rnd 11: Sc1 in each stitch around. (42)

Rnd 12: *Sc5, sc2tog*, repeat from * to * around. (36)

Rnd 13: Sc1 in each stitch around. (36)

Rnd 14: *Sc4, sc2tog*, repeat from * to * around. (30)

Rnd 15: Sc1 in each stitch around. (30)

Rnd 16: *Sc3, sc2tog*, repeat from * to * around. (24)

Rnd 17: Sc1 in each stitch around. (24)

Rnd 18: *Sc2, sc2tog*, repeat from * to * around. (18) Attach the safety eyes to the head between Rnd 13 and Rnd 14. Now take a piece of the blue yarn and sew across Rnd 20 of the ears to close them off so they won't be stuffed. Stuff the head.

Rnd 19–32: Sc1 in each stitch around. (18)

Stuff the trunk lightly to keep it flexible.

Rnd 33: In back loops only, *sc1, sc2tog*, repeat from * to * around. (12)

Cut the yarn, weave through the 12 remaining stitches, pull tight, and weave in ends.

BODY

Rnd 1: Ch18, 1dc in third ch from hook, dc14, 3dc in last, continue along other side of chains, dc15, 3dc in last, sl st in first dc. (36)

Rnd 2: Ch2 (doesn't count as first stitch now and throughout), *dc17, 2dc in next*, repeat from * to * one more time, sl st in first dc. (38)

Rnd 3: Ch2, *dc18, 2dc in next*, repeat from * to * one more time, sl st in first dc. (40)

Rnd 4: Ch2, *dc19, 2dc in next*, repeat from * to * one more time, sl st in first dc. (42)

Rnd 5: Ch2, *dc20, 2dc in next*, repeat from * to * one more time, sl st in first dc. (44)

Rnd 6: Ch2, *dc21, 2dc in next*, repeat from * to * one more time, sl st in first dc. (46)

Rnd 7: Ch2, *dc22, 2dc in next*, repeat from * to * one more time, sl st in first dc. (48)

Rnd 8: Ch2, *dc23, 2dc in next*, repeat from * to * one more time, sl st in first dc. (50)

Rnd 9: Ch2, *dc24, 2dc in next*, repeat from * to * one more time, sl st in first dc. (52)

Rnd 10: Ch2, *dc25, 2dc in next*, repeat from * to * one more time, sl st in first dc. (54)

Rnd 11: Ch2, *dc26, 2dc in next*, repeat from * to * one more time, sl st in first dc. (56)

Rnd 12: Ch2, *dc27, 2dc in next*, repeat from * to * one more time, sl st in first dc. (58)

Rnd 13: Ch2, *dc28, 2dc in next*, repeat from * to * one more time, sl st in first dc. (60)

Rnd 14: Ch2, *dc29, 2dc in next*, repeat from * to * one more time, sl st in first dc. (62)

Rnd 15: Ch2, *dc30, 2dc in next*, repeat from * to * one more time, sl st in first dc. (64)

Rnd 16: Ch2, *dc31, 2dc in next*, repeat from * to * one more time, sl st in first dc. (66)

Rnd 17: Ch2, *dc32, 2dc in next*, repeat from * to * one more time, sl st in first dc. (68)

Rnd 18: Ch2, *dc33, 2dc in next*, repeat from * to * one more time, sl st in first dc. (70)

Rnd 19: Ch2, *dc34, 2dc in next*, repeat from * to * one more time, sl st in first dc. (72)

Cut a long tail to close the body in the end; fold the body in line with the increases to make the belly straight.

ARMS (MAKE 2)

Rnd 1: Start with a magic ring, 6sc in the ring. (6)
Rnd 2: 2sc in each stitch around. (12)
Rnd 3: *Sc1, 2sc in next*, repeat from * to * around. (18)
Rnd 4: *Sc2, 2sc in next*, repeat from * to * around. (24)
Rnd 5–Rnd 9: Sc1 in each stitch around. (24)
Rnd 10: *Sc2, sc2tog*, repeat from * to * around. (18)

Rnd 11–Rnd 12: Sc1 in each stitch around. (18)

Rnd 13: Sl st 1, ch2 (doesn't count as first stitch now and throughout), dc1 in each stitch around, sl st in first dc. (18)

Rnd 14: Ch2, dc2tog, dc1 in each stitch around, sl st in first dc. (17)

At this point, stuff the hand and use a small piece of the blue yarn to sew across the arm between Rnd 12 and Rnd 13.

Rnd 15: Ch2, dc1 in each stitch around, sl st in first dc. (17)

Rnd 16: Ch2, dc2tog, dc1 in each stitch around, sl st in first dc. (16)

Rnd 17: Ch2, dc1 in each stitch around, sl st in first dc. (16)

Rnd 18: Ch2, dc2tog, dc1 in each stitch around, sl st in first dc. (15)

Rnd 19: Ch2, dc1 in each stitch around, sl st in first dc. (15)

Rnd 20: Ch2, dc2tog, dc1 in each stitch around, sl st in first dc. (14)

Rnd 21: Ch2, dc1 in each stitch around, sl st in first dc. (14)

Rnd 22: Ch2, dc2tog, dc1 in each stitch around, sl st in first dc. (13)

Cut a long tail to attach the arms to the body later.

LEGS (MAKE 2)

Rnd 1: Start with a magic ring, ch2, 12dc in the ring, sl st in first dc. (12)

Rnd 2: Ch2, *dc1, 2dc in next*, repeat from * to * around, sl st in first dc. (18)

Rnd 3–Rnd 7: Ch2, dc1 in each stitch around, sl st in first dc. (18)

Cut yarn and weave in ends.

PUTTING IT ALL TOGETHER

- Place both legs between the bottom two layers of the body, and then use the remaining yarn from the body to sew across the seam, with the legs in between, to close the body and at the same time attach the legs.
- Sew an arm to each side of the body between Rnd 1 and Rnd 3.

- Sew Rnd 14 of the head (ears not included) to Rnd 1 of the body.

HORSE

Trot, trot, trot. I love to gallop and run!

DIMENSIONS

14.6 in. (37 cm) long and 6.7 in. (17 cm) wide

MATERIALS

DK #3 lightweight yarn (sample shown in Scheepjes Stone Washed):
• beige (Boulder Opal): 164 yd. (150 m)
• white (Moon Stone): 109.4 yd. (100 m)
• black (Black Onyx): 54.7 yd. (50 m)
Crochet hook: US size D-3 (3 mm)
Brown and black safety eyes, 15 mm
Black safety eyes, 10 mm (for nostrils)
Fiberfill stuffing
Yarn needle and scissors

DIFFICULTY LEVEL

FIRST EAR

Rnd 1: With beige, start with a magic ring, 6sc in the ring. (6)
Rnd 2: Sc1 in each stitch around. (6)
Rnd 3: 2sc in each stitch around. (12)
Rnd 4–Rnd 5: Sc1 in each stitch around. (12)
Rnd 6: *Sc1, 2sc in next*, repeat from * to * around. (18)
Rnd 7: Sc1 in each stitch around. (18)
Cut the thread and weave in the ends.

SECOND EAR

Rnd 1: With beige, start with a magic ring, 6sc in the ring. (6)
Rnd 2: Sc1 in each stitch around. (6)
Rnd 3: 2sc in each stitch around. (12)
Rnd 4–Rnd 5: Sc1 in each stitch around. (12)
Rnd 6: *Sc1, 2sc in next*, repeat from * to * around. (18)
Rnd 7: Sc1 in each stitch around. (18)
Do not cut the yarn!

HEAD

Crochet with the **beige** yarn of the second ear to form the top of the head.
Rnd 1: Ch9, take the first ear, sc in all 18 stitches of the first ear, sc in the other side of each of the 9 chains you just crocheted, sc in each of the 18 stitches of the second ear. (54)
Rnd 2: Sc1 in each stitch around. (54)
Rnd 3: Sc18, sc2tog, sc25, sc2tog, sc7. (52)
Rnd 4: Sc in each round stitch around. (52)
Rnd 5: Sc18, sc2tog, sc24, sc2tog, sc6. (50)
Rnd 6: Sc1 in each stitch around. (50)
Rnd 7: Sc18, sc2tog, sc23, sc2tog, sc5. (48)
Rnd 8: Sc1 in each stitch around. (48)
Rnd 9: Sc18, sc2tog, sc22, sc2tog, sc4. (46)
Rnd 10: Sc1 in each stitch around. (46)
Rnd 11: Sc18, sc2tog, sc21, sc2tog, sc3. (44)
Rnd 12: Sc1 in each stitch around. (44)
Rnd 13: Sc18, sc2tog, sc20, sc2tog, sc2. (42)
Rnd 14: Sc1 in each stitch around. (42)
Rnd 15: Sc18, sc2tog, sc19, sc2tog, sc1. (40)
Rnd 16: Sc1 in each stitch around. (40)
Rnd 17: Sc18, sc2tog, sc18, sc2tog. (38)
Rnd 18: Sc1 in each stitch around. (38)
Rnd 19: Sc2tog, sc16, sc2tog, sc18. (36)
Rnd 20: Change color to **white**, sc1 in each stitch around. (36)
Rnd 21–Rnd 24: Sc1 in each stitch around. (36)
Rnd 25: *Sc4, sc2tog*, repeat from * to * around. (30)
Rnd 26: *Sc3, sc2tog*, repeat from * to * around. (24)
Rnd 27: *Sc2, sc2tog*, repeat from * to * around. (18) Attach the brown and black safety eyes between Rnd 10 and Rnd 11 of the head; stuff the head.
Rnd 28: *Sc1, sc2tog*, repeat from * to * around. (12) Attach the black safety eyes as nostrils between Rnd 26 and Rnd 27.

Fold the seam flat and sew the front and back of the head against each other.

BODY

Rnd 1: With beige ch18, dc1 in third ch from hook, dc14, 3dc in last, continue along other side of chains, dc15, 3dc in last, sl st in first dc. (36)

Rnd 2: Ch2 (does not count as first stitch for the entire pattern), *dc17, 2dc in next*, repeat from * to * 1 more time, sl st in first dc. (38)

Rnd 3: With beige ch2, dc3, **with white** dc12, **with beige** dc3, 2dc in next, dc18, 2dc in next, sl st in first dc. (40)

Rnd 4: With beige ch2, dc3, **with white** dc13, **with beige** dc3, 2dc in next, dc19, 2dc in next, sl st in first dc. (42)

Rnd 5: With beige ch2, dc3, **with white** dc14, **with beige** dc3, 2dc in next, dc20, 2dc in next, sl st in first dc. (44)

Rnd 6: With beige ch2, dc3, **with white** dc15, **with beige** dc3, 2dc in next, dc21, 2dc in next, sl st in first dc. (46)

Rnd 7: With beige ch2, dc3, **with white** dc16, **with beige** dc3, 2dc in next, dc22, 2dc in next, sl st in first dc. (48)

Rnd 8: With beige ch2, dc3, **with white** dc17, **with beige** dc3, 2dc in next, dc23, 2dc in next, sl st in first dc. (50)

Rnd 9: With beige ch2, dc3, **with white** dc18, **with beige** dc3, 2dc in next, dc24, 2dc in next, sl st in first dc. (52)

Rnd 10: With beige ch2, dc3, **with white** dc19, **with beige** dc3, 2dc in next, dc25, 2dc in next, sl st in first dc. (54)

Rnd 11: With beige ch2, dc3, **with white** dc20, **with beige** dc3, 2dc in next, dc26, 2dc in next, sl st in first dc. (56)

Rnd 12: With beige ch2, dc3, **with white** dc21, **with beige** dc3, 2dc in next, dc27, 2dc in next, sl st in first dc. (58)

Rnd 13: With beige ch2, dc3, **with white** dc22, **with beige** dc3, 2dc in next, dc28, 2dc in next, sl st in first dc. (60)

Rnd 14: With beige ch2, dc3, **with white** dc23, **with beige** dc3, 2dc in next, dc29, 2dc in next, sl st in first dc. (62)

Rnd 15: With beige ch2, dc3, **with white** dc24, **with beige** dc3, 2dc in next, dc30, 2dc in next, sl st in first dc. (64)

Rnd 16: With beige ch2, dc3, **with white** dc25, **with beige** dc3, 2dc in next, dc31, 2dc in next, sl st in first dc. (66)

Rnd 17: With beige ch2, dc3, **with white** dc26, **with beige** dc3, 2dc in next, dc32, 2dc in next, sl st in first dc. (68)

Rnd 18: With beige ch2, dc3, **with white** dc27, **with beige** dc3, 2dc in next, dc33, 2dc in next, sl st in first dc. (70)

Rnd 19: With beige ch2, dc3, **with white** dc28, **with beige** dc3, 2dc in next, dc34, 2dc in next, sl st in first dc. (72)

Rnd 20: With beige ch2, *dc35, 2dc in next*, repeat from * to * 1 more time, sl st in first dc. (74)

Cut a long piece of yarn to close the body at the end and fold it in half on the line of increases.

ARMS (MAKE 2)

Rnd 1: With black, start with a magic ring, 6sc in the ring. (6)

Rnd 2: 2sc in each stitch around. (12)

Rnd 3: *Sc1, 2sc in next*, repeat from * to * around. (18)

Rnd 4: *Sc2, 2sc in next*, repeat from * to * around. (24)

Rnd 5: Working in back loops only, sc1 in every stitch around. (24)

Rnd 6–Rnd 9: Sc1 in each stitch around. (24)

Rnd 10: *Sc2, sc2tog*, repeat from * to * around. (18)

Rnd 11: Sc1 in each stitch around. (18)

Cut a long yarn to use after Rnd 13.

Rnd 12: With brown sl st, ch2, dc1 in each stitch around, sl st in first dc. (18)

Rnd 13: Ch2, dc2tog, dc1 in each stitch around, sl st in first dc. (17)

Fill up the hand and sew the arm shut between Rnd 11 and Rnd 12.

Rnd 14: Ch2, dc1 in each stitch around, sl st in first dc. (17)

Rnd 15: Ch2, dc2tog, dc1 in each stitch around, sl st in first dc. (16)

Rnd 16: Ch2, dc1 in each stitch around, sl st in first dc. (16)

Rnd 17: Ch2, dc2tog, dc1 in each stitch around, sl st in first dc. (15)

Rnd 18: Ch2, dc1 in each stitch around, sl st in first dc. (15)

Rnd 19: Ch2, dc2tog, dc1 in every stitch around, sl st in first dc. (14)

Rnd 20: Ch2, dc1 in each stitch around, sl st in first dc. (14)

Rnd 21: Ch2, dc2tog, dc1 in every stitch around, sl st in first dc. (13)

Cut a long tail to attach the arms later.

LEGS (MAKE 2)

Rnd 1: With black, start with a magic ring, 6sc in the ring. (6)

Rnd 2: 2sc in each stitch around. (12)

Rnd 3: *Sc1, 2sc in next*, repeat from * to * around. (18)

Rnd 4: *Sc2, 2sc in next*, repeat from * to * around. (24)

Rnd 5: Working in back loops only, sc1 in each stitch around. (24)

Rnd 6–Rnd 9: Sc1 in each stitch around. (24)

Rnd 10: *Sc2, sc2tog*, repeat from * to * around. (18)

Rnd 11: Sc1 in each stitch around. (18)

Cut a long tail to use after Rnd 13.

Rnd 12: With brown sl st, ch2, dc1 in each stitch around, sl st in first dc. (18)

Rnd 13: Ch2, dc2tog, dc1 in each stitch around, sl st in first dc. (17)

Fill up the foot and sew the leg tightly between Rnd 11 and Rnd 12.

Rnd 14: Ch2, dc1 in each stitch around, sl st in first dc. (17)

Rnd 15: Ch2, dc2tog, dc1 in each stitch around, sl st in first dc. (16)

Rnd 16: Ch2, dc1 in each stitch around, sl st in first dc. (16)

Rnd 17: Ch2, dc2tog, dc1 in each stitch around, sl st in first dc. (15)

Cut the yarn and weave in the ends.

PUTTING IT ALL TOGETHER

- Place the legs between the two layers at the bottom of the body and close the seam with the legs in between.
- Sew an arm on each side of the body between Rnd 2 and Rnd 4.
- Attach the mane by cutting pieces of white yarn of approximately 10 in. (25 cm), hold it double, insert the hook into the stitch, pull the yarn through the hole at the center, hold it on the hook, and thread the ends through the loop on the hook to make a knot. Now repeat this over the head in the part between the ears, from Rnd 2 on the forehead to Rnd 10 on the back of the head in rows of 7 to 8 stitches.
- Sew Rnd 16 of the head (ears not counted) against Rnd 1 of the body.

221

MOUSE

Cupcake and tea?

DIMENSIONS

13.8 in. (35 cm) high (including ears) and 6.7 in. (17 cm) wide

MATERIALS

DK #3 lightweight yarn (sample shown in Scheepjes Stone Washed):
• brown (Boulder Opal): 251.5 yd. (230 m)
• white (Moon Stone): 142.2 yd. (130 m)
Crochet hook: US size D-3 (3 mm)
Black and blue safety eyes, 15 mm
Pink safety nose, 15 mm wide
Fiberfill stuffing
Yarn needle and scissors

DIFFICULTY LEVEL

EARS (MAKE 2)

Rnd 1: With brown, start with a magic ring, 6sc in the ring. (6)
Rnd 2: 2sc in each stitch around. (12)
Rnd 3: *Sc1, 2sc in next*, repeat from * to * around. (18)
Rnd 4: *Sc2, 2sc in next*, repeat from * to * around. (24)
Rnd 5: *Sc3, 2sc in next*, repeat from * to * around. (30)
Rnd 6: *Sc4, 2sc in next*, repeat from * to * around. (36)
Rnd 7: *Sc5, 2sc in next*, repeat from * to * around. (42)
Rnd 8–Rnd 17: Sc1 in each stitch around. (42)
Rnd 18: Sc6, *sc2tog, sc4*, repeat from * to * 5 more times. (36)
Rnd 19: Sc6, *sc2tog, sc3*, repeat from * to * 5 more times. (30)

Rnd 20: Sc6, *sc2tog, sc2*, repeat from * to * 5 more times. (24)

Cut yarn of the first ear. When finished with the second ear, don't cut the yarn—continue with the head instructions. Fold the first ear flat after the next 3 stitches (in the center of the 6 stitches that haven't been decreased).

HEAD

Rnd 1: In second ear sc3, take the first ear and continue in the stitch after the point you folded it, sc24, continue in second ear, sc21. (48)

Rnd 2: *Sc7, 2sc in next*, repeat from * to * around. (54)

Rnd 3: Sc1 in each stitch around. (54)

Rnd 4: *Sc16, sc2tog*, repeat from * to * 2 more times. (51)

Rnd 5: Sc1 in each stitch around. (51)

Rnd 6: *Sc15, sc2tog*, repeat from * to * 2 more times. (48)

Rnd 7: Sc1 in each stitch around. (48)

Rnd 8: *Sc14, sc2tog*, repeat from * to * 2 more times. (45)

Rnd 9: Sc1 in each stitch around. (45)

Rnd 10: *Sc13, sc2tog*, repeat from * to * 2 more times. (42)

Rnd 11: Sc1 in each stitch around. (42)

Rnd 12: *Sc12, sc2tog*, repeat from * to * 2 more times. (39)

Rnd 13: Sc1 in each stitch around. (39)

Rnd 14: *Sc11, sc2tog*, repeat from * to * 2 more times. (36)

Rnd 15: Sc1 in each stitch around. (36)

Rnd 16: *Sc10, sc2tog*, repeat from * to * 2 more times. (33)

Rnd 17: Sc1 in each stitch around. (33)

Rnd 18: *Sc9, sc2tog*, repeat from * to * 2 more times. (30)

Rnd 19: Sc1 in each stitch around. (30)

Rnd 20: *Sc8, sc2tog*, repeat from * to * 2 more times. (27)

Rnd 21: Sc1 in each stitch around. (27)

Rnd 22: *Sc7, sc2tog*, repeat from * to * 2 more times. (24)

Rnd 23: Sc1 in each stitch around. (24)

Rnd 24: *Sc6, sc2tog*, repeat from * to * 2 more times. (21)

Rnd 25: Sc1 in each stitch around. (21)

Rnd 26: *Sc5, sc2tog*, repeat from * to * 2 more times. (18)

Rnd 27: Sc1 in each stitch around. (18)

Attach the safety eyes to the head between Rnd 6 and Rnd 7. Now take a piece of brown yarn and sew across the top of the head to close off the ears so they won't be stuffed. Stuff the head.

Rnd 28: *Sc1, sc2tog*, repeat from * to * around. (12) Attach the safety nose between Rnd 27 and Rnd 28. Cut the yarn, weave through the 12 remaining stitches, pull tight, and weave in ends.

BODY

Rnd 1: With brown ch18, 1dc in third ch from hook, dc14, 3dc in last, continue along other side of chains, dc15, 3dc in last, sl st in first dc. (36)

Rnd 2: Ch2 (doesn't count as first stitch now and throughout), dc3, **with white** dc11, **with brown** dc3, 2dc in next, dc17, 2dc in next, sl st in first dc. (38)

Rnd 3: With brown ch2, dc3, **with white** dc12, **with brown** dc3, 2dc in next, dc18, 2dc in next, sl st in first dc. (40)

Rnd 4: With brown ch2, dc3, **with white** dc13, **with brown** dc3, 2dc in next, dc19, 2dc in next, sl st in first dc. (42)

Rnd 5: With brown ch2, dc3, **with white** dc14, **with brown** dc3, 2dc in next, dc20, 2dc in next, sl st in first dc. (44)

Rnd 6: With brown ch2, dc3, **with white** dc15, **with brown** dc3, 2dc in next, dc21, 2dc in next, sl st in first dc. (46)

Rnd 7: With brown ch2, dc3, **with white** dc16, **with brown** dc3, 2dc in next, dc22, 2dc in next, sl st in first dc. (48)

Rnd 8: With brown ch2, dc3, **with white** dc17, **with brown** dc3, 2dc in next, dc23, 2dc in next, sl st in first dc. (50)

Rnd 9: With brown ch2, dc3, **with white** dc18, **with brown** dc3, 2dc in next, dc24, 2dc in next, sl st in first dc. (52)

Rnd 10: With brown ch2, dc3, **with white** dc19, **with brown** dc3, 2dc in next, dc25, 2dc in next, sl st in first dc. (54)

Rnd 11: With brown ch2, dc3, **with white** dc20, **with brown** dc3, 2dc in next, dc26, 2dc in next, sl st in first dc. (56)

Rnd 12: With brown ch2, dc3, **with white** dc21, **with brown** dc3, 2dc in next, dc27, 2dc in next, sl st in first dc. (58)

Rnd 13: With brown ch2, dc3, **with white** dc22, **with brown** dc3, 2dc in next, dc28, 2dc in next, sl st in first dc. (60)

Rnd 14: With brown ch2, dc3, **with white** dc23, **with brown** dc3, 2dc in next, dc29, 2dc in next, sl st in first dc. (62)

Rnd 15: With brown ch2, dc3, **with white** dc24, **with brown** dc3, 2dc in next, dc30, 2dc in next, sl st in first dc. (64)

Rnd 16: With brown ch2, dc3, **with white** dc25, **with brown** dc3, 2dc in next, dc31, 2dc in next, sl st in first dc. (66)

Rnd 17: With brown ch2, dc3, **with white** dc26, **with brown** dc3, 2dc in next, dc32, 2dc in next, sl st in first dc. (68)

Rnd 18: With brown ch2, dc3, **with white** dc27, **with brown** dc3, 2dc in next, dc33, 2dc in next, sl st in first dc. (70)

Rnd 19: With brown ch2, *dc34, 2dc in next*, repeat from * to * around, sl st in first dc. (72)

Cut a long tail to close the body in the end; fold the body in line with the increases to make the belly straight.

ARMS (MAKE 2)

Rnd 1: With white, start with a magic ring, 6sc in the ring. (6)

Rnd 2: 2sc in each stitch around. (12)

Rnd 3: *Sc1, 2sc in next*, repeat from * to * around. (18)

Rnd 4: *Sc2, 2sc in next*, repeat from * to * around. (24)

Rnd 5–Rnd 9: Sc1 in each stitch around. (24)

Rnd 10: *Sc2, sc2tog*, repeat from * to * around. (18)

Rnd 11–Rnd 12: Sc1 in each stitch around. (18)

Cut a long tail of the white yarn; you'll need it after Rnd 14.

Rnd 13: With brown sl st 1, ch2 (doesn't count as first stitch now and throughout), dc1 in each stitch around, sl st in first dc. (18)

Rnd 14: Ch2, dc2tog, dc1 in each stitch around, sl st in first dc. (17)

At this point, stuff the hand and use the yarn from Rnd 12 to sew across the arm between Rnd 12 and Rnd 13.

Rnd 15: Ch2, dc1 in each stitch around, sl st in first dc. (17)

Rnd 16: Ch2, dc2tog, dc1 in each stitch around, sl st in first dc. (16)

Rnd 17: Ch2, dc1 in each stitch around, sl st in first dc. (16)

Rnd 18: Ch2, dc2tog, dc1 in each stitch around, sl st in first dc. (15)

Rnd 19: Ch2, dc1 in each stitch around, sl st in first dc. (15)

Rnd 20: Ch2, dc2tog, dc1 in each stitch around, sl st in first dc. (14)
Rnd 21: Ch2, dc1 in each stitch around, sl st in first dc. (14)
Rnd 22: Ch2, dc2tog, dc1 in each stitch around, sl st in first dc. (13)
Cut a long tail to attach arms to body later.

LEGS (MAKE 2)

Rnd 1: With white, start with a magic ring, ch2, 12dc in the loop, sl st in first dc. (12)
Rnd 2: Ch2, *dc1, 2dc in next*, repeat from * to * around, sl st in first dc. (18)
Rnd 3: Ch2, dc1 in each stitch around, sl st in first dc. (18)
Rnd 4–Rnd 7: With brown ch2, dc1 in each stitch around, sl st in first dc. (18)
Cut yarn and weave in ends.

PUTTING IT ALL TOGETHER

- Place both legs between the bottom two layers of the body and use the remaining yarn from the body to sew across the seam, with legs in between, to close the body and at the same time attach the legs.
- Sew an arm to each side of the body between Rnd 2 and Rnd 4.
- Sew Rnd 10 of the head to Rnd 1 of the body.

PANDA

Get to know this panda, and she'll be your friend for life.

DIMENSIONS

13 in. 33 (cm) long and 6.3 in. (16 cm) wide

MATERIALS

DK #3 lightweight yarn (sample shown in Scheepjes Stone Washed):
• black (Black Onyx): 142.2 yd. (130 m)
• white (Moon Stone): 142.2 yd. (130 m)
Crochet hook: US size D-3 (3 mm)
Black and blue safety eyes, 12 mm
Black safety nose, 15 mm
wide Fiberfill stuffing
Yarn needle and scissors

DIFFICULTY LEVEL

EYES (MAKE 2)

Rnd 1: With black, start with a magic ring, 6sc in the ring. (6) *Don't pull the ring too tight; you'll put the safety eyes through the center later.*
Rnd 2: 2sc in each stitch around. (12)
Rnd 3: *Sc1, 2sc in next*, repeat from * to * around. (18)
Rnd 4: *Sc2, 2sc in next*, repeat from * to * around. (24)
Put the safety eyes though the center of Rnd 1. Don't attach the closure yet; continue with the head.

HEAD

Rnd 1: With white, start with a magic ring, 6sc in the ring. (6)

Rnd 2: 2sc in each stitch around. (12)

Rnd 3: *Sc1, 2sc in next*, repeat from * to * around. (18)

Rnd 4: *Sc2, 2sc in next*, repeat from * to * around. (24)

Rnd 5: *Sc3, 2sc in next*, repeat from * to * around. (30)

Rnd 6: *Sc4, 2sc in next*, repeat from * to * around. (36)

Rnd 7: *Sc5, 2sc in next*, repeat from * to * around. (42)

Rnd 8: *Sc6, 2sc in next*, repeat from * to * around. (48)

Rnd 9: *Sc7, 2sc in next*, repeat from * to * around. (54)

Rnd 10: *Sc8, 2sc in next*, repeat from * to * around. (60)

Rnd 11–Rnd 20: Sc1 in each stitch around. (60)

Rnd 21: *Sc8, sc2tog*, repeat from * to * around. (54)

Rnd 22: *Sc7, sc2tog*, repeat from * to * around. (48)

Rnd 23: *Sc6, sc2tog*, repeat from * to * around. (42)

Rnd 24: *Sc5, sc2tog*, repeat from * to * around. (36)

Rnd 25: *Sc4, sc2tog*, repeat from * to * around. (30)

Rnd 26: *Sc3, sc2tog*, repeat from * to * around. (24)

Rnd 27: *Sc2, sc2tog*, repeat from * to * around. (18)

Put the safety eyes through the head between Rnd 18 and Rnd 19, and attach the closures inside the head. Stuff the head, but not too firm, so you can press it flat and mold it in shape.

Rnd 28: *Sc1, sc2tog*, repeat from * to * around. (12)

Cut a long tail and sew the seam closed. Sew along the edge of the eyes with the remaining yarn.

NOSE

Rnd 1: With white, start with a magic ring, 6sc in the ring. (6)

Rnd 2: 2sc in each stitch around. (12)

Rnd 3: *Sc1, 2sc in next*, repeat from * to * around. (18)

Rnd 4: *Sc2, 2sc in next*, repeat from * to * around. (24)

Rnd 5: Sc1 in each stitch around. (24)

Cut a long tail, attach the safety nose in Rnd 3, stuff the nose, and sew the nose to the head.

EARS (MAKE 2)

Rnd 1: With black, start with a magic ring, 6sc in the ring. (6)

Rnd 2: 2sc in each stitch around. (12)

Rnd 3: *Sc1, 2sc in next*, repeat from * to * around. (18)

Rnd 4: *Sc2, 2sc in next*, repeat from * to * around. (24)

Rnd 5–Rnd 9: Sc1 in each stitch around. (24)

Cut a long tail, stuff the ears lightly, and sew an ear to each side of the head between Rnd 6 and Rnd 14.

BODY

Rnd 1: With black ch18, 1dc in third ch from hook, dc14, 3dc in last, continue along other side of chains, dc15, 3dc in last, sl st in first dc. (36)

Rnd 2: Ch2 (doesn't count as first stitch for entire pattern), *dc17, 2dc in next*, repeat from * to * one more time, sl st in first dc. (38)

Rnd 3: Ch2, *dc18, 2dc in next*, repeat from * to * one more time, sl st in first dc. (40)

Rnd 4: Ch2, *dc19, 2dc in next*, repeat from * to * one more time, sl st in first dc. (42)

Rnd 5: Ch2, *dc20, 2dc in next*, repeat from * to * one more time, sl st in first dc. (44) Cut the black yarn.

Rnd 6: With white ch2, *dc21, 2dc in next*, repeat from * to * one more time, sl st in first dc. (46)

Rnd 7: Ch2, *dc22, 2dc in next*, repeat from * to * one more time, sl st in first dc. (48)

Rnd 8: Ch2, *dc23, 2dc in next*, repeat from * to * one more time, sl st in first dc. (50)

Rnd 9: Ch2, *dc24, 2dc in next*, repeat from * to * one more time, sl st in first dc. (52)

Rnd 10: Ch2, *dc25, 2dc in next*, repeat from * to * one more time, sl st in first dc. (54)

Rnd 11: Ch2, *dc26, 2dc in next*, repeat from * to * one more time, sl st in first dc. (56)

Rnd 12: Ch2, *dc27, 2dc in next*, repeat from * to * one more time, sl st in first dc. (58)

Rnd 13: Ch2, *dc28, 2dc in next*, repeat from * to * one more time, sl st in first dc. (60)

Rnd 14: Ch2, *dc29, 2dc in next*, repeat from * to * one more time, sl st in first dc. (62)

Rnd 15: Ch2, *dc30, 2dc in next*, repeat from * to * one more time, sl st in first dc. (64)

Rnd 16: Ch2, *dc31, 2dc in next*, repeat from * to * one more time, sl st in first dc. (66)

Rnd 17: Ch2, *dc32, 2dc in next*, repeat from * to * one more time, sl st in first dc. (68)

Rnd 18: Ch2, *dc33, 2dc in next*, repeat from * to * one more time, sl st in first dc. (70)

Rnd 19: Ch2, *dc34, 2dc in next*, repeat from * to * one more time, sl st in first dc. (72)

Rnd 20: Ch2, *dc35, 2dc in next*, repeat from * to * one more time, sl st in first dc. (74)

Cut a long tail to close the body in the end.

ARMS (MAKE 2)

Rnd 1: With black, start with a magic ring, 6sc in the ring. (6)

Rnd 2: 2sc in each stitch around. (12)

Rnd 3: *Sc1, 2sc in next*, repeat from * to * around. (18)

Rnd 4: *Sc2, 2sc in next*, repeat from * to * around. (24)

Rnd 5–Rnd 9: Sc1 in each stitch around. (24)

Rnd 10: *Sc2, sc2tog*, repeat from * to * around. (18)

Rnd 11–Rnd 12: Sc1 in each stitch around. (18)

Rnd 13: Sl st 1, ch2 (doesn't count as first stitch now and thourghout), dc1 in each stitch around, sl st in first dc. (18)

Rnd 14: Ch2, dc2tog, dc1 in each stitch around, sl st in first dc. (17)

At this point, stuff the hand (not too much) and use a small piece of yarn to sew across the arm between Rnd 12 and Rnd 13.

Rnd 15: Ch2, dc1 in each stitch around, sl st in first dc. (17)

Rnd 16: Ch2, dc2tog, dc1 in each stitch around, sl st in first dc. (16)

Rnd 17: Ch2, dc1 in each stitch around, sl st in first dc. (16)

Rnd 18: Ch2, dc2tog, dc1 in each stitch around, sl st in first dc. (15)

Rnd 19: Ch2, dc1 in each stitch around, sl st in first dc. (15)

Rnd 20: Ch2, dc2tog, dc1 in each stitch around, sl st in first dc. (14)

Rnd 21: Ch2, dc1 in each stitch around, sl st in first dc. (14)

Rnd 22: Ch2, dc2tog, dc1 in each stitch around, sl st in first dc. (13)

Cut a long tail to attach arms to body in the end.

LEGS (MAKE 2)

Rnd 1: With black, start with a magic ring, ch2, 12dc in the ring, sl st in first dc. (12)

Rnd 2: Ch2, *dc1, 2dc in next*, repeat from * to * around, sl st in first dc. (18)

Rnd 3–Rnd 7: Ch2, dc1 in each stitch around, sl st in first dc. (18)

Cut yarn and weave in ends.

PUTTING IT ALL TOGETHER

- Place both legs between the bottom two layers of the body and use the remaining yarn from the body to sew across the seam, with the legs in between, to close the body and at the same time attach legs.
- Sew an arm to each side of the body between Rnd 1 and Rnd 4.
- Sew Rnd 23 of the head to Rnd 1 of the body.

PRINCESS

Every princess needs a friend.

DIMENSIONS

15 in. (38 cm) long and 5.9 in. (15 cm) wide

MATERIALS

DK #3 lightweight yarn (sample shown in Scheepjes Stone Washed):
• hair color (Yellow Jasper): 109.4 yd. (100 m)
• pink (Corondum Ruby): 164 yd. (150 m)
• red (Red Jasper): 54.7 yd. (50 m)
• skin color (Softfun 2466): 87.5 yd. (80 m)
Crochet hook: US size D-3 (3 mm)
Black and blue safety eyes, 12 mm
Small amount of fiberfill stuffing
Yarn needle and scissors

DIFFICULTY LEVEL

HAIR AND HEAD

Rnd 1: With hair color, start with a magic ring, 6sc in the ring. (6)
Rnd 2: 2sc in each stitch around. (12)
Rnd 3: *Sc1, 2sc in next*, repeat from * to * around. (18)
Rnd 4: *Sc2, 2sc in next*, repeat from * to * around. (24)
Rnd 5–Rnd 8: Sc1 in each stitch around. (24)
Rnd 9: *Ch6, sc in second ch from hook, sc4, continue in Rnd 8, sc12*, repeat from * to * one more time. (34)
You will now continue in both sides of the chains and the bun to form the top of the head.
Rnd 10: * **In first side of chains**, sc5; **in other side of chains**, 4sc in next, sc4; **in bun**, sc12*, repeat from * to * one more time. (50)
Rnd 11–Rnd 15: Sc1 in each stitch around. (50)
Rnd 16: Sc17, **with skin color** sc1, **with hair color** sc32. (50)
Rnd 17: Sc17, **with skin color** sc3, **with hair color** sc30. (50)
Rnd 18: Sc17, **with skin color** sc5, **with hair color** sc28. (50)
Rnd 19: Sc16, **with skin color** sc8, **with hair color** sc26. (50)
Rnd 20: Sc15, **with skin color** sc11, **with hair color** sc24. (50)
Rnd 21: Sc14, **with skin color** sc14, **with hair color** sc22. (50)
Rnd 22: Sc13, **with skin color** sc17, **with hair color** sc20. (50)
Rnd 23: Sc12, **with skin color** sc20, **with hair color** sc18. (50)

Rnd 24: Sc11, **with skin color** sc23, **with hair color** sc16. (50)
Rnd 25: Sc10, **with skin color** sc40. (50)
Cut the hair color yarn.
Rnd 26: *Sc6, sc2tog*, repeat from * to * to last 2 stitches, sc2. (44)
Rnd 27: *Sc5, sc2tog*, repeat from * to * to last 2 stitches, sc2. (38)
Rnd 28: *Sc4, sc2tog*, repeat from * to * to last 2 stitches, sc2. (32)
Rnd 29: *Sc3, sc2tog*, repeat from * to * to last 2 stitches, sc2. (26)
Rnd 30: *Sc2, sc2tog*, repeat from * to * to last 2 stitches, sc2. (20)
Attach eyes between Rnd 22 and Rnd 23 with 10 stitches between them and stuff the head.
Rnd 31: *Sc1, sc2tog*, repeat from * to * to last 2 stitches, sc2. (14)
Cut a long tail, fold the opening horizontally, and sew the seam closed.

BODY

Rnd 1: With pink ch18, dc in 3rd ch from hook, dc14, 3dc in last, continue along other side of chains, dc15, 3dc in last, sl st in first dc. (36)
Rnd 2: Ch2 (doesn't count as first stitch for entire pattern), *dc17, 2dc in next*, repeat from * to * one more time, sl st in first dc. (38)
Rnd 3: Ch2, *dc18, 2dc in next*, repeat from * to * one more time, sl st in first dc. (40)
Rnd 4: Ch2, *dc19, 2dc in next*, repeat from * to * one more time, sl st in first dc. (42)
Rnd 5: With red ch2, dc9, bow (*ch3, 3dc in same st as ch3, ch2, sl st in same st as 3dc*, rep from * to *), dc11, 2dc in next, dc20, 2dc in next, sl st in first dc. (44)
Cut the red yarn.
Rnd 6: With pink ch2, dc9, **now dc1 around the center of the bow into the stitch below**, dc11, 2dc in next, dc21, 2dc in next, sl st in first dc. (46)
Rnd 7: Ch2, *dc22, 2dc in next*, repeat from * to * one more time, sl st in first dc. (48)
Rnd 8: Ch2, *dc23, 2dc in next*, repeat from * to * one more time, sl st in first dc. (50)
Rnd 9: Ch2, *dc24, 2dc in next*, repeat from * to * one more time, sl st in first dc. (52)
Rnd 10: Ch2, *dc25, 2dc in next*, repeat from * to * one more time, sl st in first dc. (54)
Rnd 11: Ch2, *dc26, 2dc in next*, repeat from * to * one more time, sl st in first dc. (56)

Rnd 12: Ch2, *dc27, 2dc in next*, repeat from * to * one more time, sl st in first dc. (58)

Rnd 13: Ch2, *dc28, 2dc in next*, repeat from * to * one more time, sl st in first dc. (60)

Rnd 14: Ch2, *dc29, 2dc in next*, repeat from * to * one more time, sl st in first dc. (62)

Rnd 15: Ch2, *dc30, 2dc in next*, repeat from * to * one more time, sl st in first dc. (64)

Rnd 16: Ch2, *dc31, 2dc in next*, repeat from * to * one more time, sl st in first dc. (66)

Rnd 17: Ch2, *dc32, 2dc in next*, repeat from * to * one more time, sl st in first dc. (68)

Rnd 18: Ch2, *dc33, 2dc in next*, repeat from * to * one more time, sl st in first dc. (70)

Rnd 19: Ch2, *dc34, 2dc in next*, repeat from * to * one more time, sl st in first dc. (72)

Rnd 20: In front loops only, ch1, *skip 2, 7dc in next, skip 2, sc1*, repeat from * to * around, sl st in first ch. (12 scallops)

Rnd 21: Attach red yarn in unworked back loops of Rnd 19, ch2, *dc35, 2dc in next*, repeat from * to * one more time, sl st in first dc. (74)

Cut the pink yarn.

Rnd 22: Ch2, *dc36, 2dc in next*, repeat from * to * one more time, sl st in first dc. (76)

Cut a long tail to close the body and attach the feet in the end.

FEET (MAKE 2)

Rnd 1: With red, start with a magic ring, 6sc in the ring. (6)

Rnd 2: 2sc in each stitch around. (12)

Rnd 3: *Sc1, 2sc in next*, repeat from * to * around. (18)

Rnd 4: With skin color sc3, **with red** sc15. (18)

Rnd 5: With skin color sc4, **with red** sc14. (18)

Rnd 6: With skin color sc5, **with red** sc13. (18)

Rnd 7–Rnd 8: With skin color sc1 in each stitch around. (18)

Cut yarn, weave in ends, and stuff feet lightly.

ARMS (MAKE 2)

Rnd 1: With skin color, start with a magic ring, 6sc in the ring. (6)

Rnd 2: 2sc in each stitch around. (12)

Rnd 3: *Sc1, 2sc in next*, repeat from * to * around. (18)

Rnd 4–Rnd 10: Sc1 in each stitch around. (18)

Cut a long tail to use after Rnd 12.

Rnd 11: With pink sl st 1, ch2, dc1 in each stitch around, sl st in first dc. (18)

Rnd 12: Ch2, dc2tog, dc1 in each stitch around, sl st in first dc. (17)

Now stuff the hand and sew across the arm between Rnd 10 and Rnd 11.

Rnd 13: Ch2, dc1 in each stitch around, sl st in first dc. (17)

Rnd 14: Ch2, dc2tog, dc1 in each stitch around, sl st in first dc. (16)

Rnd 15: Ch2, dc1 in each stitch around, sl st in first dc. (16)

Rnd 16: Ch2, dc2tog, dc1 in each stitch around, sl st in first dc. (15)

Rnd 17: Ch2, dc1 in each stitch around, sl st in first dc. (15)

Rnd 18: Ch2, dc2tog, dc1 in each stitch around, sl st in first dc. (14)

Rnd 19: Ch2, dc1 in each stitch around, sl st in first dc. (14)

Cut a long tail to attach arms to body in the end.

CROWN

With red, ch30 (or number of chains that will fit around the bun), sl st in first ch to close the circle, sc1, hdc1, in next: (ch1, dc1, ch1, tr1, ch1, dc1, ch1), hdc1, sc1, and sew to princess's bun.

PUTTING IT ALL TOGETHER

- Place the feet between the bottom two layers of the body and use the remaining yarn from the body to sew across the seam, with the feet in between, to close the body and at the same time attach the feet.
- Sew an arm to each side of the body, between Rnd 1 and Rnd 4.
- Sew Rnd 27 of the head to Rnd 1 of the body.

PUG

Puppies love to snuggle in their cozy beds.

DIMENSIONS

12.2 in. (31 cm) long and 6.3 in. (16 cm) wide

MATERIALS

DK #3 lightweight yarn (sample shown in Scheepjes Stone Washed):
• beige (Boulder Opal): 164 yd. (150 m)
• black (Black Onyx): 87.5 yd. (80 m)
Optional: small scrap of red for bow
Crochet hook: US size D-3 (3 mm)
Brown and black safety eyes, 15 mm
Black or brown safety nose, 15 mm wide
Small amount of fiberfill stuffing
Yarn needle and scissors

DIFFICULTY LEVEL

EARS (MAKE 2)

Rnd 1: With black, start with a magic ring, 6sc in the ring. (6)
Rnd 2: Sc1 in each stitch around. (6)
Rnd 3: 2sc in each stitch around. (12)
Rnd 4: *Sc1, 2sc in next*, repeat from * to * around. (18)
Rnd 5: *Sc2, 2sc in next*, repeat from * to * around. (24)
Rnd 6–Rnd 7: Sc1 in each stitch around. (24)
Rnd 8: *Sc2, sc2tog*, repeat from * to * around. (18)
Rnd 9–Rnd 12: Sc1 in each stitch around. (18)
Cut a long tail and don't weave in the ends.

HEAD

Rnd 1: With beige, ch9, take first ear, sc in each of the 18 stitches of first ear, sc in each of the 9 chains you just made, sc in each of the 18 stitches of second ear. (54; this means you'll count first 9 chains, first ear, 9 sc, and second ear)

Note: Keep tails of ears on the outside of the head; you'll use them later.

Rnd 2–Rnd 5: Sc1 in each stitch around. (54)

Rnd 6: Sc10, **with black** sc3, **with beige** sc38, **with black** sc3. (54)

Rnd 7: With beige sc10, **with black** sc4, **with beige** sc37, **with black** sc3. (54)

Rnd 8: With black sc1, **with beige** sc9, **with black** sc5, **with beige** sc36, **with black** sc3. (54)

Rnd 9: With black sc2, **with beige** sc8, **with black** sc9, **with beige** sc29, **with black** sc6. (54)

Rnd 10: With black sc3, **with beige** sc8, **with black** sc9, **with beige** sc28, **with black** sc6. (54)

Rnd 11: With black sc3, **with beige** sc9, **with black** sc8, **with beige** sc29, **with black** sc5. (54)

Rnd 12: With black sc3, **with beige** sc10, **with black** sc7, **with beige** sc30, **with black** sc4. (54)

Rnd 13: With black sc3, **with beige** sc11, **with black** sc6, **with beige** sc31, **with black** sc3. (54)

Rnd 14: With black sc3, **with beige** sc4, sc2tog, *sc7, sc2tog*, repeat from * to * to end. (48)

Cut the black yarn.

Rnd 15: *Sc6, sc2tog*, repeat from * to * around. (42)

Rnd 16: *Sc5, sc2tog*, repeat from * to * around. (36)

On each of the ears you still have a thread hanging; use it to sew through both sides of the ears between Rnd 12 of the ear and Rnd 1 of the head so the ear won't get stuffed. After that, fold the ear like it's folded in the pictures and sew it in place with the remaining yarn, and weave in the remaining ends. Attach safety eyes between Rnd 11 and Rnd 12 of the head.

Rnd 17: *Sc4, sc2tog*, repeat from * to * around. (30)

Rnd 18: *Sc3, sc2tog*, repeat from * to * around. (24)

Rnd 19: *Sc2, sc2tog*, repeat from * to * around. (18) Stuff the head.

Rnd 20: *Sc1, sc2tog*, repeat from * to * around. (12) Fold seam flat and sew front and back of the head together; weave in the ends.

NOSE

Rnd 1: With black ch6, sc1 in second ch from hook, sc3, 3sc in last, continue along other side of chains, sc4, 3sc in last. (14)

Rnd 2: *Sc6, 5sc in next*, repeat from * to * around. (22)

Rnd 3: Sc6, 3sc in next, sc8, 3sc in next, sc6. (26)

Rnd 4–Rnd 5: Sc1 in each stitch around. (26)

Cut a long tail, attach safety nose in center of Rnd 3, stuff nose, and sew to head.

BODY

Rnd 1: With beige ch18, 1dc in third ch from hook, dc14, 3dc in last, continue along other side of chains, dc15, 3dc in last, sl st in first dc. (36)

Rnd 2: Ch2 (doesn't count as first stitch for entire pattern), *dc17, 2dc in next*, repeat from * to * one more time, sl st in first dc. (38)

Rnd 3: Ch2, *dc18, 2dc in next*, repeat from * to * one more time, sl st in first dc. (40)

Rnd 4: Ch2, *dc19, 2dc in next*, repeat from * to * one more time, sl st in first dc. (42)

Rnd 5: Ch2, *dc20, 2dc in next*, repeat from * to * one more time, sl st in first dc. (44)

Rnd 6: Ch2, *dc21, 2dc in next*, repeat from * to * one more time, sl st in first dc. (46)

Rnd 7: Ch2, *dc22, 2dc in next*, repeat from * to * one more time, sl st in first dc. (48)

Rnd 8: Ch2, *dc23, 2dc in next*, repeat from * to * one more time, sl st in first dc. (50)

Rnd 9: Ch2, *dc24, 2dc in next*, repeat from * to * one more time, sl st in first dc. (52)

Rnd 10: Ch2, *dc25, 2dc in next*, repeat from * to * one more time, sl st in first dc. (54)

Rnd 11: Ch2, *dc26, 2dc in next*, repeat from * to * one more time, sl st in first dc. (56)

Rnd 12: Ch2, *dc27, 2dc in next*, repeat from * to * one more time, sl st in first dc. (58)

Rnd 13: Ch2, *dc28, 2dc in next*, repeat from * to * one more time, sl st in first dc. (60)

Rnd 14: Ch2, *dc29, 2dc in next*, repeat from * to * one more time, sl st in first dc. (62)

Rnd 15: Ch2, *dc30, 2dc in next*, repeat from * to * one more time, sl st in first dc. (64)

Rnd 16: Ch2, *dc31, 2dc in next*, repeat from * to * one more time, sl st in first dc. (66)

Rnd 17: Ch2, *dc32, 2dc in next*, repeat from * to * one more time, sl st in first dc. (68)

Rnd 18: Ch2, *dc33, 2dc in next*, repeat from * to * one more time, sl st in first dc. (70)

Rnd 19: Ch2, *dc34, 2dc in next*, repeat from * to * one more time, sl st in first dc. (72)

Rnd 20: Ch2, *dc35, 2dc in next*, repeat from * to * one more time, sl st in first dc. (74)

Cut a long tail to close the body in the end.

ARMS (MAKE 2)

Rnd 1: With beige, start with a magic ring, 6sc in the loop. (6)

Rnd 2: 2sc in each stitch around. (12)

Rnd 3: *Sc1, 2sc in next*, repeat from * to * around. (18)

Rnd 4: *Sc2, 2sc in next*, repeat from * to * around. (24)

Rnd 5–Rnd 9: Sc1 in each stitch around. (24)

Rnd 10: *Sc2, sc2tog*, repeat from * to * around. (18)

Rnd 11–Rnd 12: Sc1 in each stitch around. (18)

Rnd 13: Sl st 1, ch2 (doesn't count as first stitch now and throughout), dc1 in each stitch around, sl st in first dc. (18)

Rnd 14: Ch2, dc2tog, dc1 in each stitch around, sl st in first dc. (17)

At this point, stuff the hand (not too much) and use a small piece of yarn to sew across the arm between Rnd 12 and Rnd 13.

Rnd 15: Ch2, dc1 in each stitch around, sl st in first dc. (17)

Rnd 16: Ch2, dc2tog, dc1 in each stitch around, sl st in first dc. (16)

Rnd 17: Ch2, dc1 in each stitch around, sl st in first dc. (16)

Rnd 18: Ch2, dc2tog, dc1 in each stitch around, sl st in first dc. (15)

Rnd 19: Ch2, dc1 in each stitch around, sl st in first dc. (15)

Rnd 20: Ch2, dc2tog, dc1 in each stitch around, sl st in first dc. (14)

Rnd 21: Ch2, dc1 in each stitch around, sl st in first dc. (14)

Rnd 22: Ch2, dc2tog, dc1 in each stitch around, sl st in first dc. (13)

Cut a long tail to attach the arms to the body in the end.

LEGS (MAKE 2)

Rnd 1: With beige, start with a magic ring, ch2, 12dc in the ring, sl st in first dc. (12)

Rnd 2: Ch2, *dc1, 2dc in next*, repeat from * to * around, sl st in first dc. (18)

Rnd 3–Rnd 7: Ch2, dc1 in each stitch around, sl st in first dc. (18)

Cut yarn and weave in the ends.

TAIL

Rnd 1: With beige, start with a magic ring, 6sc in the ring. (6)

Rnd 2: 2sc in each stitch around. (12)

Rnd 3–Rnd 30: Sc1 in each stitch around. (12) Tie a knot in the tail and weave in the ends.

BOW (OPTIONAL)

With red, start with a magic ring, *ch3, 6tr in the loop, ch3, sl st in ring*, repeat from * to * one more time.

Cut a long tail, wrap it around the center of the bow a few times, and tie a knot on the back of the bow. Leave a tail to attach later.

PUTTING IT ALL TOGETHER

- Place both legs and tail between the bottom two layers of the body. Use the remaining yarn from the body and sew across the seam, with the legs and the tail in between, to close and at the same time attach all parts.
- Sew an arm to each side of the body between Rnd 1 and Rnd 4.
- Sew Rnd 15 of the head (not counting ears) to Rnd 1 of the body.
- Optional: Sew bow to the left ear.

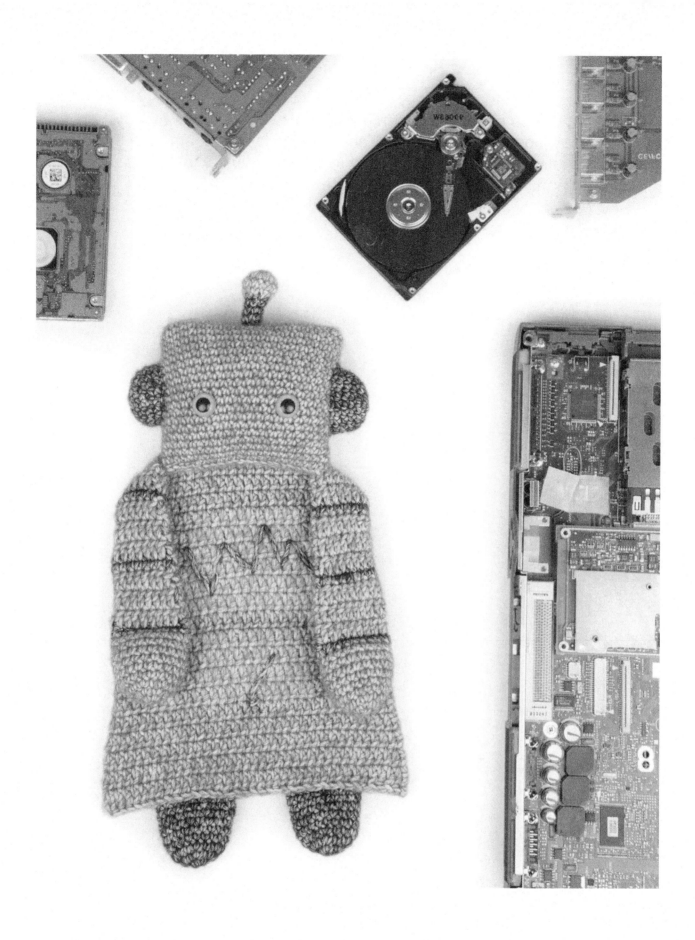

ROBOT

Beep! Beep! Come and see what I can do!

DIMENSIONS

11.8 in. (30 cm) long and 6.3 in. (16 cm) wide

MATERIALS

DK #3 lightweight yarn (sample shown in Scheepjes Stone Washed):
• gray (Smokey Quartz): 164 yd. (150 m)
• black (Black Onyx): 87.5 yd. (80 m)
• blue (Green Agate): 87.5 yd. (80 m)
Crochet hook: US size D-3 (3 mm)
Black and blue safety eyes, 12 mm
Small amount of fiberfill stuffing
Yarn needle and scissors

DIFFICULTY LEVEL

HEAD

Rnd 1: With gray ch21, sc1 in second ch from hook, sc18, 4sc in last, continue along other side of chains, sc18, 4sc in last. (45)
Rnd 2–Rnd 20: Sc1 in each stitch around. (45)
Attach safety eyes between Rnd 12 and Rnd 13 with 9 stitches in between.
Cut a long tail, fold the opening horizontally, and sew the seam half closed. Stuff the head and sew closed to the end.

BODY

Rnd 1: With gray ch18, 1dc in third ch from hook, dc14, 3dc in last, continue along other side of chains, dc15, 3dc in last, sl st in first dc. (36)

Rnd 2: Ch2 (doesn't count as first stitch for entire pattern), *dc17, 2dc in next*, repeat from * to * one more time, sl st in first dc. (38)

Rnd 3: Ch2, *dc18, 2dc in next*, repeat from * to * one more time, sl st in first dc. (40)

Rnd 4: Ch2, *dc19, 2dc in next*, repeat from * to * one more time, sl st in first dc. (42)

Rnd 5: Ch2, dc4, **with blue** dc12, **with gray** dc4, 2dc in next, dc20, 2dc in next, sl st in first dc. (44)

Rnd 6: Ch2, dc4, **with blue** dc13, **with gray** dc4, 2dc in next, dc21, 2dc in next, sl st in first dc. (46)

Rnd 7: Ch2, dc4, **with blue** dc14, **with gray** dc4, 2dc in next, dc22, 2dc in next, sl st in first dc. (48)

Rnd 8: Ch2, dc4, **with blue** dc15, **with gray** dc4, 2dc in next, dc23, 2dc in next, sl st in first dc. (50)

Rnd 9: Ch2, dc4, **with blue** dc16, **with gray** dc4, 2dc in next, dc24, 2dc in next, sl st in first dc. (52)

Rnd 10: Ch2, dc4, **with blue** dc17, **with gray** dc4, 2dc in next, dc25, 2dc in next, sl st in first dc. (54)

Rnd 11: Ch2, dc4, **with blue** dc3, **with gray** dc12, **with blue** dc3, **with gray** dc4, 2dc in next, dc26, 2dc in next, sl st in first dc. (56)

Rnd 12: Ch2, dc4, **with blue** dc2, **with gray** dc2, **with blue** dc11, **with gray** dc2, **with blue** dc2, **with gray** dc4, 2dc in next, dc27, 2dc in next, sl st in first dc. (58)

Rnd 13: Ch2, dc4, **with blue** dc2, **with gray** dc2, **with blue** dc12, **with gray** dc2, **with blue** dc2, **with gray** dc4, 2dc in next, dc28, 2dc in next, sl st in first dc. (60)

Rnd 14: Ch2, dc4, **with blue** dc2, **with gray** dc2, **with blue** dc13, **with gray** dc2, **with blue** dc2, **with gray** dc4, 2dc in next, dc29, 2dc in next, sl st in first dc. (62)

Rnd 15: Ch2, dc4, **with blue** dc2, **with gray** dc2, **with blue** dc14, **with gray** dc2, **with blue** dc2, **with gray** dc4, 2dc in next, dc30, 2dc in next, sl st in first dc. (64)

Cut the blue yarn.

Rnd 16: Ch2, *dc31, 2dc in next*, repeat from * to * one more time, sl st in first dc. (66)

Rnd 17: Ch2, *dc32, 2dc in next*, repeat from * to * one more time, sl st in first dc. (68)

Rnd 18: Ch2, *dc33, 2dc in next*, repeat from * to * one more time, sl st in first dc. (70)

Rnd 19: Ch2, *dc34, 2dc in next*, repeat from * to * one more time, sl st in first dc. (72)

Rnd 20: Ch2, *dc35, 2dc in next*, repeat from * to * one more time, sl st in first dc. (72)

Cut a long tail to close the body in the end.

ARMS (MAKE 2)

Rnd 1: With gray, start with a magic ring, 6sc in the ring. (6)

Rnd 2: 2sc in each stitch around. (12)

Rnd 3: *Sc1, 2sc in next*, repeat from * to * around. (18)

Rnd 4–Rnd 9: Sc1 in each stitch around. (18)

Rnd 10: With black sl st 1, ch1 (doesn't count as first stitch, now and throughout), sc1 in each stitch around, sl st in first sc. (18)

Rnd 11: With gray ch2, dc2tog, dc1 in each stitch around, sl st in first dc. (17)

Stuff the hand and sew across the arm between Rnd 9 and Rnd 10.

Rnd 12: Ch2, dc1 in each stitch around, sl st in first dc. (17)

Rnd 13: Ch2, dc2tog, dc1 in each stitch around, sl st in first dc. (16)

Rnd 14: With black ch1, sc1 in each stitch around, sl st in first sc. (16)

Rnd 15: With gray ch2, dc2tog, dc1 in each stitch around, sl st in first dc. (15)

Rnd 16: Ch2, dc1 in each stitch around, sl st in first dc. (15)

Rnd 17: Ch2, dc2tog, dc1 in each stitch around, sl st in first dc. (14)

Rnd 18: With black ch1, sc1 in each stitch around, sl st in first sc. (14)

Rnd 19: With gray ch2, dc2tog, dc1 in each stitch around, sl st in first dc. (13)

Rnd 20: Ch2, dc1 in each stitch around, sl st in first dc. (13)

Cut a long tail to attach the arms to the body in the end.

FEET (MAKE 2)

Rnd 1: With black, start with a magic ring, 6sc in the ring. (6)

Rnd 2: 2sc in each stitch around. (12)

Rnd 3: *Sc1, 2sc in next*, repeat from * to * around. (18)

Rnd 4–Rnd 9: Sc1 in each stitch around. (18)

Cut tail, weave in ends, and stuff feet lightly.

EARS (MAKE 2)

Rnd 1: With black, start with a magic ring, 6sc in the ring. (6)

Rnd 2: 2sc in each stitch around. (12)

Rnd 3: *Sc1, 2sc in next*, repeat from * to * around. (18)

Rnd 4–Rnd 5: Sc1 in each stitch around. (18)

Cut a long tail to attach the ears to the head later; stuff lightly.

ANTENNA

Rnd 1: With blue, start with a magic ring, 6sc in the ring. (6)

Rnd 2: 2sc in each stitch around. (12)

Rnd 3: Sc1 in each stitch around. (12)

Cut tail and stuff the top.

Rnd 4: With black sc2tog 6 times. (6)

Rnd 5–Rnd 8: Sc1 in each stitch around. (6)

Cut a long tail to attach to the head in the end.

PUTTING IT ALL TOGETHER

- Start by putting together the head: Sew an ear to each side of the head between Rnd 6 and Rnd 15. Sew the antenna to the top of the head.
- With black yarn, embroider a graph on the top screen of the robot and an indicator on the bottom screen. I like to embroider by first making the entire line and then going backward through the line as shown in the picture.
- Place the feet between the bottom two layers of the body and use the remaining yarn from the body to sew across the seam, with the feet in between, to close the body and at the same time attach the feet.
- Sew an arm to each side of the body, between Rnd 1 and Rnd 4.
- Sew Rnd 17 of the head to Rnd 1 of the body.

UNICORN

Join me in the land where dreams come true!

DIMENSIONS

14.6 in. (37 cm) long and 6.7 in. (17 cm) wide

MATERIALS

DK #3 lightweight yarn (sample shown in Scheepjes Stone Washed):
• pink (Corondum Ruby): 164 in. (150 m)
• white (Moon Stone): 109.4 in. (100 m)
• black (Black Onyx): 54.7 in. (50 m)
• yellow (Yellow Jasper): 32.8 in. (30 m)
• various colors for the mane
Crochet hook: US size D-3 (3 mm)
Brown and black safety eyes, 15 mm
Black safety eyes, 10 mm (for nostrils)
Small amount of fiberfill stuffing
Yarn needle and scissors

DIFFICULTY LEVEL

INSTRUCTIONS

To make the unicorn, follow the instructions for the horse on pages 107–9, but replace beige with pink yarn and add a few strands of different colors into the mane. Finally, hook the horn as follows to complete the unicorn.

HORN

Rnd 1: With yellow, start with a magic ring, 6sc in the ring. (6)
Rnd 2: Sc1 in each stitch around. (6)

Rnd 3: 2sc in each stitch around. (12)
Rnd 4–Rnd 5: Sc1 in each stitch around. (12)
Rnd 6: *Sc1, 2sc in next*, repeat from * to * around. (18)
Rnd 7–Rnd 11: Sc1 in each stitch around. (18)
Cut a long tail, stuff the horn, and sew the horn to the forehead from Rnd 3 to Rnd 8.

CLOTHES
FOR YOUR DOLLS

CLOTHES
FOR THE RAGDOLLS

These ragdolls also want to look extra cute occasionally, so crochet them a few special pieces to wear!

MATERIALS

- DK weight yarn. I used Scheepjes Soft Fun (different colors); each item of clothing can be hooked with 1 ball (140 m)
- Crochet hook: US size G-6 (4 mm)
- Yarn needle and scissors

SPECIAL STITCHES

- V-stitch (v-st) = dc, ch1, dc in same stitch
- Double v-stitch = 2dc, ch1, 2dc in same stitch

DIFFICULTY LEVEL

PINK DRESS
(FITS STANDARD-SIZE DOLL)

Rnd 1: Ch30, sl st in the first ch to form a ring. Ch2 (does not count as the first stitch here and throughout), *dc10, 3dc in the next stitch, dc3, 3dc in the next stitch*, repeat from * to * once more, sl st in the first dc. (38)

Rnd 2: Ch2, dc11, ch8, skip 7 dc, dc12, ch8, skip 7 dc, dc1, sl st in first dc. (40)

Rnd 3: Ch2, dc1 in each stitch around, sl st in first dc. (40)

Rnd 4: Ch2, dc15, 2dc in next stitch, dc19, 2dc in next stitch, dc4, sl st in first dc. (42)

Rnd 5: Ch2, dc16, 2dc in next stitch, dc10, [Bow: ch4, 3dc in first of ch4, ch3, sl st in same as 3dc, ch3, 3dc in same as 3dc, ch3, sl st in same as 3dc], 10dc, 2dc in next stitch, dc4, sl st in first dc. (44)

Rnd 6: Ch2, dc17, 2dc in next stitch, dc10, dc1 around the center of the bow in the stitch below, dc10, 2dc in next stitch, dc4, sl st in first dc. (46)

Rnd 7: Ch2, 1 v-st in same as ch2, skip 1 dc, *1 v-st in next dc, skip 1 dc*, repeat from * to * around, sl st in first dc of first v-st. (23 v-st)

Rnd 8–Rnd 9: Sl st in the ch-1 space of the first v-st, ch2, 1 v-st in same as ch2, 1 v-st in ch-1 space of each v-st around, sl st in first dc of first v-st. (23 v-st)

Rnd 10: Sl st in ch-1 space of the first v-st, ch2, 1 double v-st in same as ch2, 1 double v-st in ch-1 space of each v-st around, sl st in first dc of first double v-st. (23 double v-st)

Rnd 11–Rnd 13: Sl st in ch-1 space of the first double v-st, ch2, 1 double v-st in same as ch2, 1 double v-st in ch-1 space of every double v-st around, sl st in first dc of first double v-st. (23 double v-st)

Rnd 14: Sl st in ch-1 space of the first double v-st, ch2, 5dc in same as ch2, 5dc in ch-1 space of each double v-st around, sl st in first dc. (23 groups of 5dc)
Cut the yarn and weave in the ends.

RED DRESS
(FITS STANDARD-SIZE DOLL)

Rnd 1: Ch30, sl st in first ch to make a ring. Ch2 (doesn't count as first stitch now and throughout), *dc10, 3dc in next stitch, dc3, 3dc in next stitch*, repeat from * to * once more, sl st in first dc. (38)

Rnd 2: Ch2, dc11, ch8, skip 7 dc, dc12, ch8, skip 7 dc, dc1, sl st in first dc. (40)

Rnd 3: Ch2, dc1 in each stitch around, sl st in first dc. (40)

Rnd 4: Ch2, dc15, 2dc in next stitch, dc19, 2dc in next stitch, dc4, sl st in first dc. (42)

Rnd 5: Ch2, dc16, 2dc in next stitch, dc10, [Bow: ch4, 3dc in first of ch4, ch3, sl st in same as 3dc, ch3, 3dc in same as 3dc, ch3, sl st in same as 3dc], dc10, 2dc in next stitch, dc4, sl st in first dc. (44)

Rnd 6: Ch2, dc17, 2dc in next stitch, dc10, dc1 around the center of the bow in the stitch below, dc10, 2dc in next stitch, dc4, sl st in first dc. (46)

Rnd 7: Ch2, dc18, 2dc in next stitch, dc22, 2dc in next stitch, dc4, sl st in first dc. (48)

Rnd 8: Ch2, dc19, 2dc in next stitch, dc23, 2dc in next stitch, dc4, sl st in first dc. (50)

Rnd 9: Ch2, dc20, 2dc in next stitch, dc24, 2dc in next stitch, dc4, sl st in first dc. (52)

Rnd 10: Ch2, dc21, 2dc in next stitch, dc25, 2dc in next stitch, dc4, sl st in first dc. (54)

Rnd 11: Ch2, dc22, 2dc in next stitch, dc26, 2dc in next stitch, dc4, sl st in first dc. (56)

Rnd 12: Ch2, dc23, 2dc in next stitch, dc27, 2dc in next stitch, dc4, sl st in first dc. (58)

Rnd 13: Ch2, dc24, 2dc in next stitch, dc28, 2dc in next stitch, dc4, sl st in first dc. (60)

Rnd 14: Ch2, dc25, 2dc in next stitch, dc29, 2dc in next stitch, dc4, sl st in first dc. (62)

Rnd 15: Ch2, dc26, 2dc in next stitch, dc30, 2dc in next stitch, dc4, sl st in first dc. (64)

Rnd 16: Ch2, dc27, 2dc in next stitch, dc31, 2dc in next stitch, dc4, sl st in first dc. (66)

Cut yarn and weave in ends.

PEACH DRESS

(FITS MINI DOLL)

Rnd 1: Ch20, sl st in first ch to make a ring. Ch2 (doesn't count as first stitch now and throughout), *dc6, 3dc in next stitch, dc2, 3dc in next stitch*, repeat from * to * once more, sl st in first dc. (28)

Rnd 2: Ch2, dc7, ch7, skip 6 dc, dc8, ch7, skip 6 dc, dc1, sl st in first dc. (30)

Rnd 3: Ch2, dc1 in each stitch around, sl st in first dc. (30)

Rnd 4: Ch2, dc10, 2dc in next stitch, dc7, [Bow: ch4, 3dc in first of ch4, ch3, sl st in same as 3dc, ch3, 3dc in same as 3dc, ch3, sl st in same as 3dc], dc7, 2dc in next stitch, dc4, sl st in first dc. (32)

Rnd 5: Ch2, dc11, 2dc in next stitch, dc7, dc1 around the center of the bow in the stitch below, dc7, 2dc in next stitch, dc4, sl st in first dc. (34)

Rnd 6: Ch2, 1 v-st in same as ch2, skip 1 dc, *1 v-st in next dc, skip 1 dc*, repeat from * to * around, sl st in first dc of first v-st. (17 v-st)

Rnd 7: Sl st in the ch1-space of the first v-st, ch2, 1 v-st in same as ch2, 1 v-st in the ch1-space of each v-st around, sl st in first dc of first v-st. (17 v-st)

Rnd 8: Sl st in the ch1-space of the first v-st, ch2, 1 double v-st in same as ch2, 1 double v-st in the ch1-space of each v-st around, sl st in first dc of first double v-st. (17 double v-st)

Rnd 9: Sl st in the ch1-space of the first double v-st, ch2, 5dc in same as ch2, 5dc in the ch1-space of each double v-st around, sl st in first dc. (17 groups of 5dc)

Cut yarn and weave in ends.

Rnd 1: Ch20, sl st in first ch to make a ring. Ch2 (doesn't count as first stitch now and throughout), *dc6, 3dc in next stitch, dc2, 3dc in next stitch*, repeat from * to * once more, sl st in first dc. (28)

Rnd 2: Ch2, dc7, ch7, skip 6 dc, dc8, ch7, skip 6 dc, dc1, sl st in first dc. (30)

Rnd 3: Ch2, dc1 in each stitch around, sl st in first dc. (30)

Rnd 4: Ch2, dc10, 2dc in next stitch, dc7, [Bow: ch4, 3dc in first of ch4, ch3, sl st in same as 3dc, ch3, 3dc in same as 3dc, ch3, sl st in same as 3dc], dc7, 2dc in next stitch, dc4, sl st in first dc. (32)

Rnd 5: Ch2, dc11, 2dc in next stitch, dc7, dc1 around the center of the bow in the stitch below, dc7, 2dc in next stitch, dc4, sl st in first dc. (34)

Rnd 6: Ch2, dc12, 2dc in next stitch, dc16, 2dc in next stitch, dc4, sl st in first dc. (36)

Rnd 7: Ch2, dc13, 2dc in next stitch, dc17, 2dc in next stitch, dc4, sl st in first dc. (38)

Rnd 8: Ch2, dc14, 2dc in next stitch, dc18, 2dc in next stitch, dc4, sl st in first dc. (40)

Rnd 9: Ch2, dc15, 2dc in next stitch, dc19, 2dc in next stitch, dc4, sl st in first dc. (42)

Cut yarn and weave in ends.

DARK BLUE SWEATER

(FITS STANDARD-SIZE DOLL)

Rnd 1: Ch30, sl st in first ch to make a ring. Ch2 (doesn't count as first stitch now and throughout), *dc10, 3dc in nextstitch, dc3, 3dc in next stitch*, repeat from * to * once more, sl st in first dc. (38)

Rnd 2: Ch2, dc11, ch8, skip 7 dc, dc12, ch8, skip 7 dc, dc1, sl st in first dc. (40)

Rnd 3: Ch2, dc14, 2dc in next stitch, dc19, 2dc in next stitch, dc5, sl st in first dc. (42)

Rnd 4: Ch2, dc15, 2dc in next stitch, dc20, 2dc in next stitch, dc5, sl st in first dc. (44)

Rnd 5: Ch2, dc16, 2dc in next stitch, dc21, 2dc in next stitch, dc5, sl st in first dc. (46)

Rnd 6: Ch2, dc17, 2dc in next stitch, dc22, 2dc in next stitch, dc5, sl st in first dc. (48)

Rnd 7: Ch2, dc18, 2dc in next stitch, dc23, 2dc in next stitch, dc5, sl st in first dc. (50)

Rnd 8: Ch2, dc19, 2dc in next stitch, dc24, 2dc in next stitch, dc5, sl st in first dc. (52)

Cut yarn and weave in ends.

SLEEVES (MAKE 2)

Rnd 1: Attach yarn in the first ch of Rnd 2. Ch2 (doesn't count as first stitch now and throughout), dc8, dc1 in the side of the next dc of Rnd 2, continue in the skipped stitch of Rnd 1: dc7, dc1 in the side of the next dc of Rnd 2, sl st in first dc. (17)

Rnd 2–Rnd 7: Ch2, dc1 in each stitch around, sl st in first dc. (17)

Cut yarn and weave in ends. Repeat for second sleeve.

LIGHT BLUE SWEATER

(FITS MINI DOLL)

Rnd 1: Ch20, sl st in first ch to make a ring. Ch2 (doesn't count as first stitch now and throughout), *dc6, 3dc in next stitch, dc2, 3dc in next stitch*, repeat from * to * once more, sl st in first dc. (28)

Rnd 2: Ch2, dc7, ch7, skip 6 dc, dc8, ch7, skip 6 dc, dc1, sl st in first dc. (30)

Rnd 3: Ch2, dc10, 2dc in next stitch, dc14, 2dc in next stitch, dc4, sl st in first dc. (32)

Rnd 4: Ch2, dc11, 2dc in next stitch, dc15, 2dc in next stitch, dc4, sl st in first dc. (34)

Rnd 5: Ch2, dc12, 2dc in next stitch, dc16, 2dc in next stitch, dc4, sl st in first dc. (36)

Cut yarn and weave in ends.

SLEEVES (MAKE 2)

Rnd 1: Attach yarn in the first ch of Rnd 2, ch2 (doesn't count as first stitch now and throughout), dc7, dc1 in the side of the next dc of Rnd 2, continue in the skipped stitch of Rnd 1: dc6, dc1 in the side of the next dc of Rnd 2, sl st in first dc. (15)

Rnd 2–Rnd 5: Ch2, dc1 in each stitch around, sl st in first dc. (15)

Cut yarn and weave in ends. Repeat for second sleeve.

VISUAL INDEX

Bunny

Baby Bunny

Crocodile

Baby Crocodile

Dog

Puppy

Fox

Kit

Frog

Baby Frog

Hippo

Hippo Calf

Kangaroo

Joey

Monkey

Baby Monkey

Owl

Owlet

Penguin

Baby Penguin

Sheep

Lamb

OTHER ANIMALS AND FRIENDS

Calico Cat

Elephant

Horse

Mouse

Panda

Princess

Pug

Robot

CLOTHES FOR YOUR DOLLS

Unicorn

Pink Dress

Red Dress

Peach Dress

Yellow Dress

Dark Blue Sweater

Light Blue Sweater

Printed in Great Britain
by Amazon

37967438R00156